REEF FISHES

CORALS AND INVERTEBRATES OF

The Caribbean

A Diver's Guide

ELIZABETH WOOD & LAWSON WOOD

PASSPORT BOOKS

NTC/Contemporary Publishing Group

First published in 2001 by
Passport Books, a division of
NTC/Contemporary Publishing Group, Inc.
4255 West Touhy Avenue
Lincolnwood (Chicago), Illinois 60712–1975
U.S.A.

Copyright © 2000 in text: Elizabeth Wood
Copyright © 2000 in photographs: Lawson
Wood

Copyright © 2000 New Holland Publishers
(UK) Ltd

10 9 8 7 6 5 4 3 2 1

All rights reserved. No part of this publication may be reproduced, stored in a retrieval
system or transmitted, in any form or by any
means, electronic, mechanical, photocopy-
ing, recording or otherwise, without the prior
permission of NTC/Contemporary Publishing
Group, Inc.

ISBN 0–658–01309–2

Library of Congress Catalog Card Number:
On file

Published in conjunction with New Holland
Publishers (UK) Ltd

Publishing Manager: Jo Hemmings
Project Editor: Michaella Standen
Copy-editor and Indexer: Martyn Yeo
Designer: Chris Aldridge
Production Controller: Joan Woodroffe

Reproduction by Modern Age Repro House
Limited, Hong Kong
Printed and bound in Singapore by Kyodo
Printing Co (Singapore) Pte Ltd

Photographer's Acknowledgements

Lesley Orson, Helmut Debelius, Paul
Humann, Ned DeLoach, Catherine Leech,
Sean Robinson, Alan Marquardt, Michael &
Karyn Allard, Aggressor Fleet International,
Captain Don's Habitat, Cleveland Williams,
UNEXSO, Linton & Polly Tibbetts, Morris
Kevan International, McCluskey & Associates,
BGB & Associates, Axis Management, Bet &
Bill Bithray, Sea & Sea, Nikon, Fuji, KJP, The
Shark Group, Eastern Visual Communications,
Michaella Standen, Harlequin Travel.

Author's Acknowledgements

Thanks to the many without whose help this
publication would not have been possible; in
particular: Paul Humann; Helmut Debelius; Les-
ley Orson; Linton Tibbetts; Tom Carrick, Trinidad
& Tobago Tourist Board; Bahamas Tourist
Board; Cayman Islands Tourist Board; Bermuda
Tourism Authority; Antigua & Barbuda Tourism
Authority; Honduras Tourist Office; St.Kitts &
Nevis Tourist Board; Mexican Tourist Board;
Turks & Caicos Tourist Office; McCluskey &
Associates; Trimaran Cuan Law; Aggressor Fleet
International; Captain Don's Habitat, Bonaire &
Curacao; Anse Chastanet,St.Lucia; KJP & Fuji
Film; Eastern Photocolour Limited; Sea & Sea
Limited; The Shark Group. Coral code repro-
duced by kind permission of the Marine Con-
servation Society (www.mcsuk.org).

CONTENTS

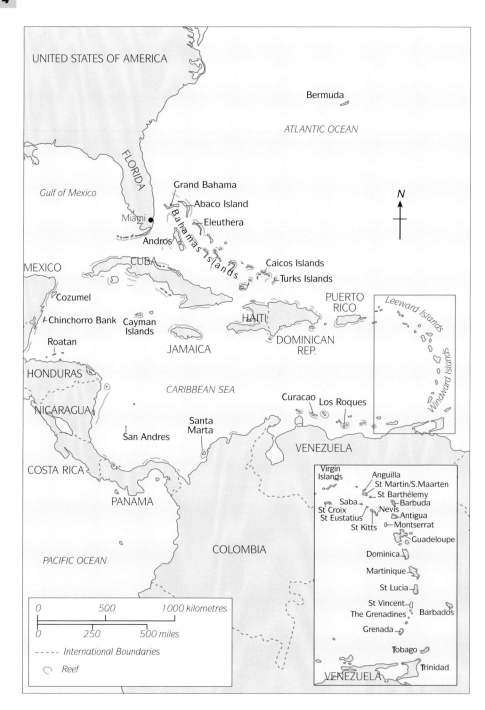

UNITED STATES OF AMERICA

Bermuda

ATLANTIC OCEAN

FLORIDA

Gulf of Mexico

Grand Bahama

Abaco Island

Miami

Eleuthera

Bahamas Islands

Andros

N

MEXICO

CUBA

Caicos Islands

Turks Islands

Cozumel

Chinchorro Bank

Cayman Islands

PUERTO RICO

Leeward Islands

Roatan

HAITI

JAMAICA

DOMINICAN REP.

Windward Islands

HONDURAS

CARIBBEAN SEA

Curacao   Los Roques

NICARAGUA

Santa Marta

San Andres

VENEZUELA

COSTA RICA

Virgin Islands

Anguilla

St Martin/S.Maarten

St Barthélemy

PANAMA

Saba

St Croix

Nevis

Barbuda

St Eustatius

St Kitts

Antigua

Montserrat

Guadeloupe

PACIFIC OCEAN

COLOMBIA

Dominica

Martinique

St Lucia

0	500	1000 kilometres

St Vincent

The Grenadines   Barbados

0	250	500 miles

Grenada

- - - - International Boundaries

Tobago

Reef

VENEZUELA

Trinidad

Caribbean reefs are unique structures built from the calcareous skeletons of corals and other organisms.

How Reefs Form

The basic building blocks of most Caribbean reefs are stony corals. 'Stony' refers to the limestone skeleton produced by coral polyps. The reason why these simple creatures can build huge reefs is because their living tissues contain symbiotic algae (zooxanthellae), which provide them with extra energy and enable them to lay down their skeleton more quickly and effectively.

Occasionally calcareous algae rather than corals form the main bulk of shallow reefs, occurring as pinkish-coloured nodules or sheets, which build up in solid layers. Algal reefs flourish, especially in very wave-swept areas where corals have difficulty in surviving – for example in Bermuda. On deep reefs, where coral growth tails off, calcareous algae are responsible for most of the reef building. These are very obvious on many of the drop-offs in the Caribbean.

Fragments of mollusc and crab shells, corals and calcareous algae contribute to reef formation by filling in holes and irregularities. Undigested material that has passed through the gut of coral-feeding animals does not go to waste either. Tons of sand and fragments reach the surface of the reef in this way, and the fragments become chemically bonded or cemented together to help form a rigid but porous structure. While calcareous forms provide solid material for the reef, soft-bodied organisms such as sponges play useful roles by binding coral rubble together to form larger, more stable pieces. They also help to fix these pieces to the bottom.

Types of Reef

Fringing reefs: The commonest type of reef found in the Caribbean is the fringing reef, which develops close to the shore of mainland coastlines and tropical islands and in evolutionary terms is relatively 'young'. Fringing reefs may be very shallow, but in places where the seabed drops away steeply close to the shore they can be hundreds of metres deep. Features include terraces, gentle slopes, spurs, canyons, pinnacles and steep-sided faces. Many of the region's fringing reefs drop downward in a series of steps or terraces, rather than as a continuous slope or drop-off. In some places the steps are so wide that the entire inner (landward) part of each one is covered by sand and coral debris. In this way, an inner and outer terrace are formed, separated by hundreds of metres or even several kilometres of sandy seabed.

Barrier Reefs

Barrier reefs typically occur on the outer edge of the continental shelf, where the seabed drops abruptly from one or two hundred metres to the deep ocean floor beneath. Some barriers have evolved from fringing reefs, whose position relative to the land has changed; others have a more complicated geological history. Barrier reefs of any size are present only off Belize, Yucatan and the Bahamas. The former is the largest – it is about 30km (19 miles) from the shore and over 260km (160 miles) long.

Atolls

'True' atolls occur in oceanic waters, beyond the edge of the continental shelf. The foundation is volcanic rock, on which lies a cap of coral limestone thousands of metres thick, with living coral on the very top. Darwin's widely accepted theory is that each atoll started life millions of years ago as a fringing reef around a volcanic island peak. Over time, the island gradually subsided, but the reef kept on growing, forming a circular structure with a lagoon in the middle. About 400 atolls exist in the world's tropical oceans, but few of these are in the Caribbean region. Glover's Reef and two adjacent reefs in

Typical 'ironstone' shoreline and blowhole.

Belize, surrounded by water 350 to 1,000m (1,150 to 3,280ft) deep, are considered to be true atolls. So too is the isolated Hogsty Reef in the Bahamas, in water over 1,800m (5,905ft) deep. Cay Sal Bank, also in the Bahamas, is probably a drowned atoll. There are a number of other, atoll-like formations, some of which (for instance, Alacran Reef and Chincharro Bank in Mexico) occur on, rather than beyond, the continental shelf and are therefore known as shelf atolls. They look like oceanic atolls, but differ from Darwin's description because they do not have a volcanic foundation.

Other Reef Formations

There are many other reef formations, ranging in size from a few metres to hundreds or thousands of metres in diameter. Pinnacles are tall and narrow, generally with a diameter of 50m (165ft) or less, and occur either in atoll lagoons or on the slope of outer reefs. Patch reefs may also stand tens of metres above the seabed, but are relatively wide. Large ones (several kilometres in diameter) are often called platform reefs. Bank reefs are similar to platform reefs but their tops may be as much as 40m (130ft) below the surface of the water, with no parts emerging. They may represent 'drowned reefs', and are quite numerous in the Caribbean region. Underwater caves or blue holes occur in places such as the Bahamas and Belize. These are eroded sink holes formed during periods of lowered sea level, and then flooded with seawater.

Sand Cays

In many cases, patch reefs break the surface and islands are formed. This happens when waves breaking on the top of the reef produce debris, which is then swept on to the reef flat, where it accumulates. Shingle ramparts or banks often build up on the windward edge, while a sandy islet forms on the sheltered side. These patch reefs are then usually referred to as sand cay reefs or simply cays.

Reef Zones

The following main zones can be recognized on most reefs:

Back reef: A shallow, sheltered zone between the shore and the lagoon or seaward reef.

Typical habitats include seagrass beds, rubble and sand patches, eroded limestone slabs and small coral outcrops.

Lagoon: A mostly sandy-floored area between the back reef and the inner reef flat of barrier reefs or atolls. Depth is up to 100m (330ft). Typical habitats include sand, seagrass beds, rubble and limestone slabs, coral micro-atolls, knolls, pinnacles and patch reefs.

Reef flat: An extremely shallow (less than 1m (3ft) deep) inter-tidal area between the lagoon and the seaward reef front. This zone may be extensive on some barrier reefs and atolls, with large areas exposed at low tide. Typical habitats include seagrass beds, coral-filled tide-pools, coral micro-atolls and eroded limestone platforms with sand, rubble and small live corals.

Spillways, channels and passages: Spillways are very shallow; they drain the reef flat, but are not permanently open. Channels and passages connect the lagoon to the open sea. They vary in width and depth but are open at all states of the tide. Typical habitats include passage walls, often with rich reef life and, in contrast, the gully floor, which is often scoured and bare.

Shallow fore-reef: This is the upper part of the seaward-facing reef, to about 15 to 20m (49 to 66ft) depth. The reef may curve gently or steeply, and sometimes there are steps or terraces present. Typical habitats include algal ridges, spur and groove formations, coral and rock outcrops and sand patches. This is usually the area with the highest diversity and cover of reef building corals.

Deep fore-reef: This includes the lower part of the seaward-facing reef, from about 15 to 20m (49 to 66ft) downwards. The slope may be gentle or steep and typical habitats include walls, sand and rubble chutes, underhangs, ledges, caves and canyons.

Classification – What's in a Name?

Common names are used as much as possible throughout this book, but be aware that some species have more than one common name and this may lead to confusion. Other organisms do not even have a common name. On the other hand, the scientific name is unique and, however difficult to pronounce or remember, cannot be muddled with anything else.

A scientific name has two parts – the genus first, followed by the species. Organisms that are not sexually compatible, but have many close similarities, are placed in the same genus. Sometimes a genus has only a single species in it, but usually there are several. For example, most of the larger groupers are in the genus *Epinephelus*, while other members of the family have slightly different features and are put into other genera, such as *Cephalopholis* and *Serranus*.

Coral mounds and sand channel at Cayman Brac

The species name completes the description and identifies an entity in which individuals are sexually compatible and produce fertile offspring. Most of the larger and more obvious plants and animals from Caribbean reefs have been identified to species, but where there is uncertainty or the organism has not yet been described by taxonomists it will simply be called, for example, *Agelas* sp.

The scientific names are based on Latin or Greek, and are conventionally written in italics. The scientists who describe the species select a name, which may be descriptive of the organism concerned, named after the person who found it, or the geographic location or habitat where it was first found. The common name is sometimes a translation of the scientific name – thus *Octopus vulgaris* is the common octopus.

Reef Conservation and the Tourist

It is well known that coral reefs around the world are facing considerable threats and that many have been damaged, degraded and over-exploited. There are numerous ways in which this can happen. Activities on land are to blame in some cases. Corals and other reef inhabitants have been damaged and killed by dirty and polluted water and by sediment. Coastal developments and runoff from the land are common causes of pollution and silting. Sewage and other organic wastes are also causing particular problems for reefs.

Destructive fishing methods, anchoring and boat collisions are also taking their toll. Corals are slow growing and if damaged or removed may take years to recover. The reef environment is also being changed, degraded and destroyed by coastal developments, harbours, jetties and sea walls. Reef tourism brings benefits such as employment and foreign currency, but reefs are suffering from trampling, anchors and other impacts from intensive use.

Many reefs have been over-fished, and destructive fishing methods are wasteful and also damage the reef habitat. Equally worrying is the fact that reefs seem to be becoming more susceptible to disease, perhaps partly because of the stress they are under. On top of all these woes comes coral bleaching, which in most cases is associated with thermal stress – and is probably related to global warming caused by human-induced atmospheric pollution.

Much will be lost if reefs become further damaged. Their value as fishing grounds, sources of medicinal compounds, tourist attractions, natural self-repairing breakwaters and places of scientific interest will disappear. Many people depend on healthy reefs to make a livelihood, and their prosperity and way of life could be put in jeopardy if reef health and productivity decline.

A successful tourist industry relies on healthy reefs if it is to prosper. Yet tourism can easily damage the resource on which it depends. As tourists, we can do quite a bit to help reefs by acting responsibly and supporting conservation organizations such as the Marine Conservation Society, a UK-based charity, which produces the following Coral Code:

Planning your Holiday/ Making Choices

● When you book your holiday, try to choose a destination where active reef management is in place – such as a marine park.
● Ask your tour operator if they have an environmental policy. Enquire if – and how – they support reef conservation.
● Find out whether the tour operators explain the do's and don'ts to people before they visit the reef. It has been shown that a short briefing can dramatically cut the amount of damage caused by divers and snorkellers.
● Make sure you play your part too, not just underwater but on land. Try to minimize impact for example by being sparing with freshwater, using biodegradable shampoos and disposing of litter in the correct way – even bringing it back home if necessary.

Looking for Souvenirs

● Collection of souvenirs from the reef is prohibited in many areas – please respect all local and international laws.
● Hard corals, black corals, marine turtles, queen conch, and all their products are protected under CITES (the Convention on International Trade in Endangered Species) and can be bought and sold only with a licence.
● Resist the temptation to buy other marine curios. In most cases insufficient is known about the harvesting operations to be certain they are sustainable - take the safe route and buy alternative souvenirs.

Going Paddling, Snorkelling or Diving

● Keep to designated walkways or sand channels when in shallow reef areas. Feet and fins

Little Cayman Island – one of many Caribbean localities where the value of tourism is helping to conserve the reef.

can easily break and damage the reef top.
• Maintain perfect buoyancy control when diving so as to keep clear of the reef.
• Never stand, sit or rest on living corals. Despite having hard skeletons, part or all of the colony may die from infection if the delicate outer soft tissues are injured.
• If you need to steady yourself use finger tips on bare rock - leave your gloves behind.
• Avoid kicking up sand. It may settle on corals and other reef animals and suffocate them.
• Enjoy taking a close look at reef life, but don't touch, move or molest animals for amusement or photography.
• Be satisfied with nature as it is. Fish feeding may have a place in a few selected areas but generally is not encouraged. It disrupts natural behaviour and can upset the ecological balance of species on reefs.

Using a Boat

• When visiting the reef, always use a mooring buoy, jetty or pontoon if one is provided. Urge boat operators and authorities to consider installing buoys at frequently-visited sites.
• Never anchor on corals. They are easily broken or damaged by anchors and anchor chains.
• Reconnoitre carefully before stopping. Polaroid sunglasses make it easier to pick out seabed features. Find a sand or rubble patch and drop anchor carefully. Make sure the anchor is not dragging on to the reef.

Dangers of the Reef

By and large, coral reefs are safe places to explore. Most of the accidents that occur are connected with diving procedures and equipment rather than encounters with dangerous marine life. However, it is wise to be aware of, and avoid, certain species or situations that can lead to discomfort, injury, and – very rarely – death.

The reef is a crowded place where the inhabitants compete with each other for space and where much of life revolves around eating or avoiding being eaten. There are many mechanisms for catching food and for avoiding being eaten or grown over, including the ability to bite or sting for defence and offence, and the use of chemicals that poison or deter would-be attackers. If divers happen to touch animals that deploy toxins or get in the way of fish with sharp teeth then they may regret it.

The Following Animals are Capable of Injuring Humans:

Sharks: generally only attack when divers are spearfishing or carrying bait.
Stingrays: will only sting if trodden on or caught.
Barracuda: might possibly attack in murky water if misled by reflective gear into thinking a diver is their normal prey.
Moray eels: will readily bite divers who inadvertently put their hands into their den.
Triggerfish: nesting males are aggressive and will charge and bite divers who get too close.
Jellyfish: most species have stinging tentacles but, with the exception of sea wasps (*Carybdea alata*) and Portuguese man-of-war (*Physalia physalis*), are not dangerous.
Fire coral (Millepora spp.): inflicts a painful sting if divers brush up against it.
Hydroids: although small and inconspicuous most have a painful sting.
Fireworms: will cause a strong burning sensation if touched.
Cone shells: use strong toxins to disable prey and will inject humans with it if they are handled.
Sea urchins: have spines that are toxic in some species and can cause considerable pain if they penetrate the skin.

Distribution and Features of Caribbean Reefs

The fish and invertebrates described in this book are associated with reefs found in an area stretching from Florida and the Bahamas south to Venezuela. Bermuda, out on a limb to the north, is also included. Many of the reefs lie around the margins of two large basins – the Gulf of Mexico to the north and the Caribbean Sea to the south. The average depth in these basins is 2,000m (6,560ft), and the deepest point is 7,100m (23,295ft), in the Cayman Trench.

USA, Florida and Northern Gulf of Mexico

The Florida reef tract consists of a chain of patch and bank barrier reefs running in an arc parallel with the Florida Keys and separated from them by a shallow, muddy channel 600 to

The green moray, *Gymnothorax funebris*, is one of several reef animals that will bite if provoked!

The 'boiler reefs' of Bermuda are formed from Calcareons algae which flourish in these wave-swept areas.

800m (1,970 to 2,625ft) wide. The patch reefs shelve to a depth of about 18m (59ft), then drop to a terrace at about 20m (66ft), which extends outwards to a low relief spur and groove system of the outer bank barrier. Pollution is a serious threat and the reefs are heavily used for recreation and fishing. The southern end of the Key Largo Sanctuary is one of the most popular areas with good coral formations and clear water. Coral communities also occur on outcrops of rocky seabed in the northern part of the Gulf of Mexico.

Central America

Mexico: Over 20 platform reefs occur in the south-western Gulf of Mexico. These are close to the edge of the western Atlantic tropical zone and are affected by winter cold fronts and fresh water runoff. Coral growth is not prolific, but diving is carried out around the northern reefs.

In contrast, an extensive fringing and barrier reef system runs along the north-east coast of the Yucatan Peninsula and around the offshore islands. The most popular diving area is Cozumel, which is separated from the mainland by a deep-water channel and has clear water with many coral formations. There are two shelf atolls, of which Chincharro Bank in the south east is increasingly being visited by divers.

Belize: This country has an excellent array of reefs, many in pristine condition. There is a well-developed, almost continuous barrier reef about 260km (160 miles) long at a distance of about 30km (19 miles) from the shore. This has steep faces with plentiful corals and fish. Many patch reefs and faroes (ring-shaped reefs enclosing their own lagoon) are present on the shelf between the mainland and barrier, especially in the south. A few fringing reefs occur along the coastline to the south of the barrier reef.

Three oceanic atolls (Turneffe Islands, Lighthouse Reef, Glover's Reef) are situated on a submarine ridge off the central part of the barrier. Lighthouse Reef has a huge blue hole; Glover's Reef has 700 patch reefs in the lagoon.

Honduras: Flourishing reefs occur around the Bay Islands where the water is deep and clear. The fringing and barrier reef systems around Roatan are particularly well developed, with shallow coral gardens, patch reefs, spur and groove formations, caves, tunnels and steep walls.

Nicaragua: Patch reefs, pinnacles and platforms are widespread on the central and outer part of the continental shelf away from the effects of sediment and fresh water input. The ecology of these reefs is not well known and they are not much visited.

Costa Rica: The Atlantic coast of Costa Rica is not particularly well suited for reef development, but there are a few fringing reefs and coral communities in the south.

Panama: Coral communities and fringing reefs occur along about one quarter of the coastline but are considered mostly to have passed their most active phase of growth. However, some areas have thriving corals; probably the best developed reefs are around the San Blas Islands where diving tourism is developing.

Colombia: Rivers carrying fresh water and

sediments restrict reef growth in the west, but there are reasonably well-developed fringing reefs to the east, for example, around Islas del Rosario and Santa Marta. Both these areas are visited by divers. Offshore, beyond the edge of the continental shelf to the north west are a group of islands together with barrier reefs and atolls. The southernmost island of San Andres and the Providencia Islands are popular areas to visit and dive.

Venezuela: This country has a long coastline but reef development is limited by turbid water from several major rivers. The best development is around offshore islands, including an atoll-like structure at Los Roques, 125km (80 miles) offshore, where there are more than 30 islands and 300 smaller coral reef islets surrounded by reef. Diving trips are organized from Curacao.

Caribbean Islands

Bahamas: This is an extensive archipelago situated on two limestone banks and comprising about 2,750 islands, cays and rocks. Bank barriers and fringing reefs occur along most of the windward northern and eastern coastlines (for instance, Abaco Island, Eleuthera and Inagua) and bank edges.

Excellent reefs also occur on the south side of Grand Bahama (Peterson Cay National Park), the main reef beginning about 2km (1¼ miles) offshore in 16m (52ft) depth and dropping steeply. The fringing reef on the north-east coast of Andros has a spectacular drop-off and blue holes adjacent to the deep-water inlet The Tongue of the Ocean. An atoll (Hogsty Reef) is present between Great Inagua and Acklins Island, at the southern end of the Bahamas chain, but is seldom visited because of its isolation and rough waters. Other areas in the Bahamas are heavily dived from shore-based operations and live-aboards.

Turks and Caicos: There are eight large islands and about 40 small cays lying on two shallow banks, both of which are ringed by coral reefs, which are mostly in excellent condition. Precipitous walls occur on the western side of Providenciales and West Caicos and along the edge of the Caicos Bank to South Caicos. Across the channel is Grand Turk with its westerly facing reef wall and many spectacular features.

Cuba: Extensive reefs surround this large island and its thousands of islets and cays. Many parts of the coastline have fringing reefs, especially where the island shelf is narrow. Bank barrier reefs occur further offshore where the shelf is wider, and also seaward of the four island groups that lie off the north and south coasts. The two southern archipelagos (Jardines de la Reina and Los Canarreos) stand on the edge of the island shelf and the reefs have steep drop-offs. Much of the diving is from Isla de la Juventud at the western end of Los Canarreos.

Cayman Islands: There are three limestone islands topping submarine mountain peaks. The 100m (330ft) depth contour runs close to the shore, leaving only a narrow shelf around the islands. Fringing reefs are present on the shelf, leading to two submarine terraces, the first at 8 to 10m (26 to 33ft) depth, the second at about 20m (66ft). These are sand covered in places, with the best coral along the seaward edges. The deeper terrace drops away dramatically as a very steep slope or vertical face, featuring arches and caverns. The west side of Grand Cayman

Ironshore (old eroded reef) on Curacao.

is particularly popular with divers and has numerous dive centres.

Twelve-Mile Bank, 16km (10 miles) west of Grand Cayman, depth 30 to 40m (98 to 130ft), has large coral heads rising to within 20m (66ft) of the surface and huge barrel sponges.

Jamaica: Well-developed fringing reefs occur on the north coast with dramatic scenery, including buttresses, surge channels, walls, canyons and tunnels. Most of the diving is in this area. Damage has been inflicted from pollution and by Hurricane Allen in 1980. Diverse and extensive reefs also occur along the south coast island shelf, and there are a number of offshore banks with good corals.

Dominican Republic: Conditions in many areas favour development of mangroves and other wetlands, but reefs border about ten percent of the coastline. Most are fringing and patch reefs with small barrier reefs off the east and south coasts. Several dive centres operate.

Haiti: Fringing and barrier reefs occur, but it is only recently that biological surveys have begun. One or two dive centres operate, but most reefs remain unvisited.

Puerto Rico: Reef development along most of the north coast is curtailed due to a combination of silt-laden river runoff, heavy surge and strong currents. Some fringing reefs occur in the north east, but the water is generally turbid.

Abundant reefs and coral formations occur around the islands and on shallow platforms at the eastern end of the main island. Most scuba diving centres are located in this region.

Patch and fringing reefs occur sporadically along the south coast and there are submerged reefs along the edge of the island shelf. Coral pinnacles and buttresses occur and there are some dramatic formations in the south west with pinnacles and buttresses. Steep fringing reefs also occur around the offshore Mona Islands.

Leeward Islands

British Virgin Islands: Diving is popular throughout the Virgin Islands, with a wide range of sites visited. The British Virgin Islands comprise about 40 islands, cays and rocks. Patch and fringing reefs are associated with most, and there are also several small barrier reefs, for example, on the windward side of Anegada. The reefs are relatively shallow, generally less than 20m (66ft), without extensive walls, but there are features of interest such as spur and groove formations, ledges and caverns. Coral communities also occur on boulders and rocks, and intermingle with true reefs.

US Virgin Islands: Many of the 50 islands, cays and rocks in the US Virgin Islands are in the same archipelago as the British Virgin Islands. Some of the best coral formations are in the

Coral boulder shoreline on the west end of Little Cayman Island.

channel that runs between the large islands of St Thomas and St John. Scattered fringing reefs occur elsewhere, with the exception of the north coast of St Thomas.

St Croix and its associated islands are to the south of the main group and have fine reefs. There are numerous patch and fringing reefs; a well-developed bank barrier reef at the south and south-eastern end of the island; and canyons, tunnels, walls and an underwater nature trail at Buck Island.

Anguilla: The bank barrier reef system to the east of Seal Island includes some of Anguilla's finest coral formations, with canyons and over-hangs in deeper water. This reef system reappears offshore from the north-east tip of Anguilla, with lush coral at around 24m (79ft). These areas are most popular for diving. The fragmented fringing reef, patch reefs and outer bank barrier off the south-east coast of Anguilla is less accessible due to strong easterly winds.

St Martin and St Barthélemy: St Martin has relatively shallow reefs round most coastlines. Most diving is off the south coast, around the extensive barrier reef; there is some in the north. Coral patches and fringing reefs occur on the shelf around St Barthélemy. On the windward side, algal reefs are important. Most diving is off the more sheltered southern side of the island.

Saba and St Eustatius: St Eustatius has a rocky shoreline, sandy plains and slopes with relatively shallow algal ridges and coral reefs occurring around the island. Saba is surf-swept and rocky. The fringing reef is not developed but there are many coral outcrops and formations in shallow water and a deeper coral platform off the south coast. Dramatic volcanic sea-mounts and pinnacles topped with coral are present in deeper water on the west side. The islands are popular for diving.

St Kitts and Nevis: Fringing reefs and a small bank barrier reef occur along much of the coast-line of both islands. The east side is exposed to swell, but there is scenic diving, especially on the west and south side, with pinnacles, canyons and steep walls. Reef tourism is expanding.

Antigua and Barbuda: Coral patches and stretches of fringing reef occur round both islands, mostly formed on submerged lime-stone platforms and terraces. There is a well-

Drop-off on the US Virgin Islands.

developed bank barrier system off the north, east and south coast of Antigua. This is particu-larly scenic at the southern end with a drop-off and abundant fish life. At the northern and southern ends of Barbuda are patch and fring-ing reefs dominated by elkhorn coral. On the east coast is an extensive reef system formed mainly of calcareous algae and fire coral. The reefs are in pristine condition and diving is becoming increasingly popular.

Montserrat: Numerous patch reefs occur on the narrow coastal shelf, with some deeper pin-nacles further offshore. Diving is mostly on the west and south coasts.

Guadeloupe: There are two main islands and several smaller ones to the south and south east. Coral growth is somewhat limited by storms, rainfall runoff and volcanic discharges. The bays (Culs de Sac) between the two closely situated main islands of Grand Basse Terre and Basse Terre include some of the best reef areas, especially the northern bay, which has patch reefs and a barrier reef. Diving is popular in these areas. Extensive calcareous algal reefs occur along the east coast of Grand Terre.

Windward Islands

Dominica: This is a rugged volcanic island with a narrow insular shelf leading to deep water. Coral grows (often prolifically) on boulders and rocks rather than as true reefs. The best coral growth is on the west coast, with a well-developed fringing reef around the Cabrits Peninsula. Underwater scenery is particularly dramatic towards the southern end of the island and large fish are abundant. Diving is popular at all these sites.

Martinique: Another volcanic island with little reef development (but dramatic diving) along the north-west coastline due to almost vertical rock faces, volcanic sediments and hurricanes. In the south the island shelf is wide and there are extensive bank barrier reefs along the south-east coastline. There are many dive centres.

St Lucia: Reefs occur around all coasts but are most abundant in the south east. Rich coral communities and dramatic scenery are found around the Pitons (extinct volcanoes) in the south west, and most diving is done in this region.

St Vincent, Grenada and the Grenadines: St Vincent has poorly developed reefs, probably due to continuous volcanic activity since the Ice Ages. Patch reefs, fringing reefs and bank barrier structures are distributed sporadically around the north, east and south coast of Grenada.

The Grenadines stand on a 36 to 40m (118 to 130ft) deep platform, the edge of which runs close to the northernmost and southernmost islands. This restricts development of shallow bank reefs, but provides dramatic underwater scenery such as the wall off Bequia and the bank barrier reef off the east coast of Carriacou .

Barbados: The north-east side of the island is wave battered and there is little living reef. Numerous patch and fringe reefs occur on the south and west side, occurring up to about 300m (985ft) from the shore. Further offshore, in depths of 15 to 50m (49 to 165ft) are a series of bank reefs running parallel with the shore, consisting of fossil (submerged) coral reef with living corals on top. Diving is popular, but restricted to the west coast.

Trinidad and Tobago: Trinidad and Tobago lie on the continental shelf of Venezuela and are affected by silt and fresh water brought into the Gulf of Paria by the Orinoco River. The south coast of Trinidad is particularly muddy, but reasonable coral communities occur along the north coast. Tobago has richer coral growths, such as Buccoo Reef in the north west and fringing reefs in the north east. These are the most popular diving areas.

Lesser Antilles

Netherlands Antilles: Aruba in the west lies on the continental shelf of South America; it lacks dramatic, deep drop-offs, but has well-developed reefs, especially along the south-east coast. Curacao and Bonaire are oceanic islands with fringing reef around much of the coast, leading to a terrace and precipitous drop to about 60m (195ft). Most diving is on the more sheltered western side.

KEY TO SYMBOLS

This key describes the symbols that appear at the head of each fish species description. The symbols give a quick guide for the habit, diet and habitat of each species.

Habit

 single   pairs   groups   schools

Diet

 plankton   fish   invertebrates   turtles   mammals   algae   mixed corals

Habitat

 caves   seagrass   pelagic   sand   reefs   surface water   Mangrove

This diagram illustrates the main structures of a fish referred to in the species descriptions.

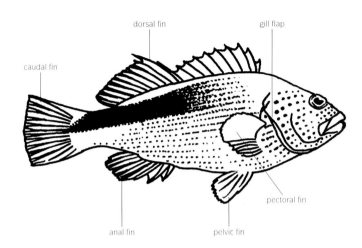

IDENTIFICATION GROUPS AND PICTORIAL GUIDE TO FAMILIES

Colour varies greatly between fish species, therefore it would seem an ideal means of identification. However, even within species, colour varies according to sex, age, region, season and surroundings. For this reason, body shape is a much more reliable means of identification. The following outlines represent the types of fish likely to be encountered in the Caribbean. Those sharing similar characteristics are grouped together for initial identification.

RAYS AND SHARKS

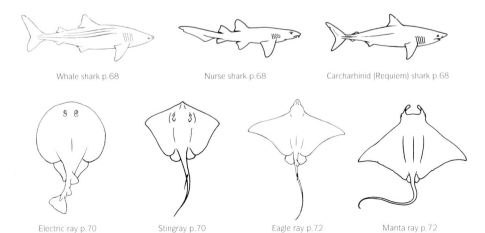

Whale shark p.68

Nurse shark p.68

Carcharhinid (Requiem) shark p.68

Electric ray p.70

Stingray p.70

Eagle ray p.72

Manta ray p.72

**SILVERY
BLADE-SHAPED FISH**

Jack p.96

Palometa p.96

SILVERY REGULAR-SHAPED FISH

Snapper p.98

Porgy p.104

Snook p.94

Chub p.106

Cardinalfish p.92

SILVERY TORPEDO-SHAPED FISH

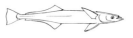

Tarpon p.74

Silversides p.76

ELONGATE FISH

Remora p.96

Trumpetfish p.80

Barracuda pp.122

SILVERY IRREGULAR-SHAPED FISH

Spadefish p.108

ELONGATE BENTHIC FISH

Pipefish p.82

Lizardfish p.76

Clingfish p.76

Tilefish p.94

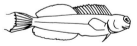

Blenny p.124

Goby p.126

Moray p.72

Snake eel p.74

Garden eel p.74

Jawfish p.122

Triplefin p.124

Clinidae p.124

IRREGULAR-SHAPED BENTHIC FISH

Toadfish p.78

Soapfish p.88

Scorpionfish p.82

Flounder p.132

Seahorse p.82

Frogfish p.78

REGULAR-SHAPED/SWIM WITH PECTORALS

Gurnard p.84

Wrasse p116

Hogfish p.116

Parrotfish p.118

COLOURFUL REGULAR-SHAPED FISH

Damselfish p.112

Basslet p.90

Hamlet p.90

Grouper p.84

Creolefish p.88

Hawkfish p.92

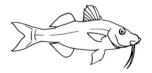

Goatfish p.106

COLOURFUL
IRREGULAR-SHAPED FISH

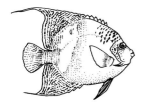

Angelfish p.110

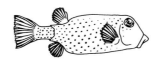

Trunkfish p.136

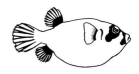

Pufferfish p.138

Porcupinefish p.138

Triggerfish p.132

Cowfish p.136

COLOURFUL
OVAL-SHAPED FISH

Surgeonfish p.130

Butterflyfish p.108

BIGEYED/CAVE-
DWELLING FISH

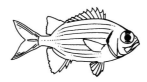

Soldierfish p.80

Squirrelfish p.80

Sweeper p.106

Bigeye p.94

SEAGRASSES

Seagrasses are the only flowering plants to occur in the sea, but the flowers are very small and inconspicuous in comparison with those produced by most land plants. For example, turtle grass flowers appear in spring and summer but are tucked away out of sight at the base of the stem and occur only in one to five per cent of all plants. The main method of spreading is by root-like rhizomes, which also anchor the plants in the sand.

1 TURTLE GRASS
Thalassia testudinum

This species has wide blades about 1cm (½in) across, which distinguish it from other seagrasses that occur in the area. Extensive swathes of turtle grass often occur in tranquil back reef lagoons, and are remarkably rich habitats to explore. The seagrass blades are often encrusted with small organisms, while flatworms, molluscs and small crabs can be found crawling around among the stems. Juveniles of various fish spend their young lives in these sheltered surroundings away from the larger reef predators. Turtle grass beds play an important ecological role because of their efficiency in removing sediment from the water. This happens because the tall leaves slow down water movement to such an extent that small particles suspended in the water no longer stay afloat but sink to the bottom.

ALGAE

Algae are widespread and common on and around reefs. Some are single celled, living by the million inside hard and soft corals. Others are filamentous or tufty, and grow as a turf on rocks and at the base of corals. These are usually grazed down like a well-kept lawn by fish, snails, sea-urchins and other grazing animals. There are, however, a number of distinctive and often strikingly beautiful species that grow on and around reefs in the area. Algae are divided into green, brown and red varieties according to the type of pigment they contain. Most of those illustrated have close relatives in other parts of the tropical world.

GREEN ALGAE

1 GREEN GRAPE ALGAE
Caulerpa racemosa

Numerous species of *Caulerpa* occur in the western Atlantic. They all have flat runners (rhizomes) and root-like rhizoids that spread out over sand, rubble or rocks and prevent the alga being dislodged. The runners give off vertical stems, which themselves bear smaller branchlets or 'leaves'. *C. racemosa* occurs both in the Indo-Pacific and western Atlantic. The tips of the branchlets are rounded and, massed together, they look like clusters of tiny green grapes. This species is common in shallow rocky areas, particularly where there is some wave surge. It grows up to 15cm (6in) tall.

2 SEA PEARL
Ventricaria ventricosa

Another interesting green alga occurring in shady places, in shallow water and to depths of well over 60m (195ft), is the sea pearl, otherwise known as sailor's eyeballs. This easily recognized alga occurs on both Indo-Pacific and Caribbean reefs. It may be solitary or in clusters, with each sphere attached by minute hair-like rhizoids. The spheres, resembling shiny marbles, are up to 5cm (2in) in diameter yet each is only a single cell – one of the largest cells known in the natural world.

1 Turtle Grass

1 Green Grape Algae

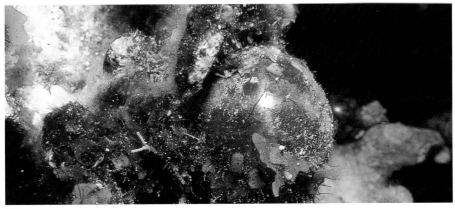

2 Sea Pearl

3 BRISTLE BALL BRUSH
Penicillus dumentosus

Penicillus species are easily recognised by their curious shape, which resembles a small shaving brush. The top of the brush in P. dumentosus is rounded (in P. pyriformis it is flat-topped) and consists of a bunch of branched, lightly calcified filaments which emerge from the top of a more heavily calcified stem. The stalk is fairly short and is firmly anchored by a mass of rhizoids that push their way down into the sand. The bristle ball brush may reach a total height of 15cm (6in). It is a common inhabitant of calm, shallow lagoons and sandy patches on reefs.

4 HANGING VINE
Halimeda copiosa

There are several species of *Halimeda* in the region. All have fronds consisting of small, round or heart-shaped disks, which are joined one to another by a narrow strand. *H. copiosa* may form long chains up to 40cm (1ft 4in) in length. It is generally found in relatively deep water of 15 to 40m (49 to 130ft) on steep or vertical faces, and hangs downwards from the holdfast. When the plants die, they turn white as the calcium deposits in their tissues are exposed. Piles of disintegrating calcified disks can often be seen adding to the accumulations of sand around reefs. Apart from being calcareous and so crunchy' for would-be grazers, *Halimeda* produces compounds (diterpenoids) that have been shown experimentally to deter fish from feeding.

5 MERMAID'S FANS
Udotea spp.

All Udotea species have flat blade-like fronds that are held stiffly and anchored into sand by a thin, root-like rhizoid. They are up to about 15cm (6in) tall. Often the frond is formed into a delicate cup. The blades are lightly or heavily calcified (depending on the species) and so feel crinkly to the touch. Calcification strengthens the blade and makes the plants less palatable to grazing fish.

6 GREEN MERMAID'S WINE GLASS
Acetabularia calyculus

This beautiful green algae consists of clumps of thin stalks about 1 to 3cm (½ to 1¼in) tall, each topped with one or several saucer-shaped, light green disks. These are up to 7mm (¼in) in diameter and are lightly calcified, with up to 30 rays radiating out from the centre. *A. calyculus* occurs in shallow water habitats that are protected from wave action, such as seagrass beds, reef and sand flats, and mangroves.

BROWN ALGAE

1 SARGASSUM SEAWEED
Sargassum fluitans

Sargassum is a fast growing brown seaweed that may form bushy growths over 1m (3ft 3in) in length. There are at least seven species in the western Atlantic, and some are so prolific as to form small forests under suitable conditions. Like other members of the genus, *S. fluitans* has small round floats or bladders along the stem. The blades or leaves of this alga have a midrib and serrated margins. It is a free-floating species often found in large clumps or rafts close to the surface of the water.

3 Bristle Ball Brush

4 Hanging Vine

5 Mermaid's Fans

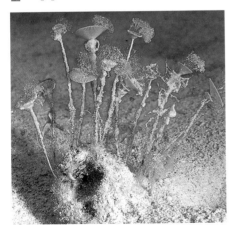

6 Green Mermaid's Wine Glass

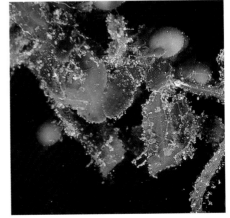

1 Sargassum Seaweed

2 Y BRANCHED ALGAE
Dictyota spp.
Dictyota occurs world-wide in most reef habitats, and there are numerous species. The plants tend to form low-lying mats up to 50cm (1ft 8in) across that spread over the surface of the reef. They occur in most habitats, but are especially common in areas sheltered from waves. All have branches that divide into two at the end, and the tips are fine and pointed in some species, rounded in others. Some *Dictyota* species have an attractive greenish or bluish sheen.

3 LEAFY ROLLED-BLADE ALGA
Padina boergesenii
Padina species have calcified fan-shaped blades with an in-rolled outer margin. *P. boergesenii* grows to about 15cm (6in) and can usually be recognized by the vertical splits in the blades. The appearance of *Padina* can vary according to the intensity with which it is being grazed. When heavily grazed by herbivorous fish, *Padina* grows close to the reef surface in a thin, branching form. However, if the fish are excluded, the algae respond rapidly. Experiments showed that within 96 hours there is a dramatic change in growth form to a rapidly growing upright blade. This form is extremely susceptible to fish grazing, but it is very competitive and may even outgrow and kill corals. *P. boergesenii* occurs widely in many habitats, but is especially common in shallow, sheltered situations.

4 WHITE SCROLL ALGA
Padina jamaicensis
This species used to be called *P. sanctae-crucis*, and its identification is still uncertain. It grows to about 15cm (6in) and has a characteristically pale appearance, due to deposits of calcium carbonate on the upper surface of the blade. As in other species of *Padina*, the concentric lines on the blade are formed from rows of microscopic hairs alternating with reproductive structures. *P. jamaicensis* is a common alga that occurs in many habitats but is especially abundant on shallow reef flats.

RED ALGAE

1 FLAT BRANCHED THICKET ALGAE
Galaxaura marginata
This species of *Galaxaura* can be distinguished from others in the same genus by the flattened blades with slightly thickened margins. These branch regularly, forming a dense clump. Close examination reveals faint, close-set lines running across the blades near their tips. This alga forms growths up to about 14cm (6in) tall which are attached by a single holdfast to rocks or other hard substrata. It occurs throughout the region in shallow, sheltered areas such as back reefs and and lagoons.

2 CRUSTOSE CORALLINE ALGAE
Rhodophyta spp.
Throughout the reef, a number of genera and many species of calcareous red algae can be found. Typically they form thin, calcareous crusts, which follow the contours of the rock. Other growth forms range from solid nodules to dense masses of criss-crossing branches. It is common to come across specimens living free on the surface of the sand, in the same way as corals. On steep slopes these algae may become plate-like with free outer edges, sometimes overlapping like tiles. They are usually either brownish, dark red or burgundy, often with white margins. Calcareous algae may dominate reef surfaces in certain situations, for example they may be so abundant in wave-exposed shallow areas that they build a ridge (algal crest) where the water breaks. One of the most important genera is *Porolithon*, sometimes known as 'reef cement'.

2 Y Branched Algae

3 Leafy Rolled-blade Alga

4 White Scroll Alga

1 Flat Branched Thicket Algae

2 Crustose Coralline Algae

INVERTEBRATES

SPONGES

Sponges are varied and abundant on western Atlantic reefs, and are generally bigger and heavier than their Indo-Pacific counterparts, especially on outer reefs. They have no sensory or nervous system and no specialized internal organs, but despite their simplicity are extremely successful animals that have colonized the seas for millions of years. They are effective filtering machines, using tiny whip-like flagellae to create a current flow and draw water into the body through small pores. Plankton, micro-organisms and small particles of debris are removed for food, and the water then exits through a hole called the osculum. This excurrent opening is invariably larger than the ingoing pores, and is usually situated at the highest point of the animal, so that waste water is more effectively carried away.

1 BRANCHING TUBE SPONGE
Pseudoceratina crassa
P. crassa has a solid base from which protrude a number of branching tubes. The sponge is up to about 45cm (1ft 6in) high and its surface is covered with numerous small bumps. There is a large exhalent opening at the top of each tube, and other openings scattered throughout. The inside of these openings is yellowish while the outside colour ranges from yellow to purple and greenish. It is common throughout the region.

2 STOVE-PIPE SPONGE
Aplysina archeri
This species can usually be identified by its long, slender tubes, which are soft and thin-walled. They may grow singly or in clusters and can be up to nearly 2m (6ft 6in) high. The inside is usually pale, while the outside is purplish or greyish. This species is quite common on deeper reefs in the Caribbean, but seen less often further north, around the Bahamas.

3 YELLOW TUBE SPONGE
Aplysina fistularis
A. fistularis consists of soft, thick-walled, yellow-orange tubes that grow up to 1.2m (4ft) high and are grouped together, joined at the base. Distinctive, finger-like growths are often present around the upper rim of each tube, but may be absent in specimens occurring in deeper water. The yellow tube sponge occurs in many reef habitats and is abundant on reefs of the Caribbean, common in the Bahamas, but seen less frequently in Florida.

4 BROWN TUBE SPONGE
Agelas conifera
A. conifera also has tubes arranged in clusters, and grows up to about 1m (3ft 3in) in height. The tubes are uneven and pitted on the outside, although they have quite a soft smooth texture. They are brownish in colour on the outside and paler inside. This species is common on reefs in the Caribbean and Bahamas, especially on walls at depths below 10m (33ft), but is seen less frequently in Florida.

5 ROW PORE ROPE SPONGE
Aplysina cauliformis
This species of *Aplysina* is one of a number of sponges that have long branches resembling thick rope. It ranges from red to purple in colour and may reach over 2.4m (8ft) in length. The distinguishing feature is that the exhalent pores are arranged in long rows down the length of the 'ropes'. This sponge is common throughout the Caribbean and Bahamas on shady slopes and walls, but only occasionally found in Florida.

6 ERECT ROPE SPONGE
Amphimedon compressa
Unlike some of the other species that occur as 'ropes', the branches of this species are erect, growing upwards from the reef surface to over 1m (3ft 3in) in height. The exhalent openings are randomly distributed, and the surface of the sponge is smooth. This sponge is usually bright red in colour, sometimes maroon, and is common throughout the region.

1 Branching Tube Sponge

2 Stove-pipe Sponge

3 Yellow Tube Sponge

4 Brown Tube Sponge

5 Row Pore Rope Sponge

6 Erect Rope Sponge

7 AZURE VASE SPONGE

Callyspongia plicifera

This sponge can be distinguished by its beautiful light blue to purple colour and the close-set ridges and valleys that cover the outside. It grows to a height of about 45cm (1ft 6in) and may occur as a single vase, or a clump of two or three together. It is common in the Caribbean, and can be seen occasionally elsewhere in the region, generally at depths of 6 to 25m (20 to 80ft).

8 PINK VASE SPONGE

Niphates digitalis

N. digitalis is pinkish to grey and resembles *C. plicifera*, although it is smaller, being less than 30cm (12in) tall, and has a rim with coloured fringes joined by almost transparent tissue. The inner surface is smooth but the outside is rough and often colonized by tiny colonial anemones (*Parazoanthus*). This sponge is found on coral reefs throughout the region, although not in large numbers.

9 STRAWBERRY VASE SPONGE

Mycale laxissima

This sponge got its name from the bright red, finger-staining slime that was exuded when specimens were removed from the water for identification. It appears very dark red or even black in deep water, but flashlight restores its brilliant crimson colour. It may consist of only a single vase up to 30cm (12in) tall, or there may be several, joined at the base. It is seen occasionally throughout the region, usually encrusting a dead black coral branch on vertical shady walls at depths below 10m (33ft).

10 GIANT BARREL SPONGE

Xestospongia muta

This unmistakable species grows to about 2m (6ft 7in) in height. It grows slowly, and large specimens are probably over a hundred years old. The outside is covered with vertical ridges or knobbly protuberances. Despite their hard structure, the rim of the barrel is quite brittle and easily damaged if divers – and some have been known to do it – try to climb inside. The barrel sponge is common throughout the region (especially the Caribbean and Bahamas), usually at depths below 15m (49ft).

11 STINKER SPONGE

Ircinia felix

Ircinia felix grows to about 30cm (12in) in height and the surface is covered by numerous tiny white cones connected by white lines. It may have a concave central depression in which osculae are situated, but at other times forms irregular lobes. This sponge is very common throughout the region, from shallow water to moderate depths. Its unfortunate name derives from the foul smell it gives off when removed from the water.

12 ORANGE ELEPHANT EAR SPONGE

Agelas clathrodes

Agelas clathrodes is a huge and unmistakable sponge that is common on reef slopes and walls throughout the region. It is orange and may form mounds or encrustations 2m (6ft 7in) across. Sometimes it protrudes as a flat mass, resembling an elephant's ear. This species is generally found in areas with some water movement, and often has other organisms growing on its surface.

13 ORANGE ICING SPONGE

Mycale laevis

This encrusting species occurs on the underside of corals or around their edges. It may modify the growth of the coral but plays a useful role because it forms a protective coating that prevents boring sponges (see below) settling and burrowing into the colony from beneath. *Mycale laevis* is orange, and can be identified by its prominent exhalent openings that protrude and are transparent or whitish in colour. It is common throughout the region.

7 Azure Vase Sponge

8 Pink Vase Sponge

9 Strawberry Vase Sponge

10 Giant Barrel Sponge

11 Stinker Sponge

12 Orange Elephant Ear Sponge

13 Orange Icing Sponge

15 RED BORING SPONGE
Cliona delitrix

The visible part of this sponge appears as a reddish crust or mound over the surface of coral heads. The rest of it lies within the coral below. Boring sponges such as this use acid to excavate tiny pits in the limestone. They bore using special cells with microscopic mobile protrusions (pseudopodia or 'false feet'). The pseudopodia secrete acid and so gradually dissolve and penetrate the limestone, releasing tiny chips of coral rock. As the sponge grows it spreads inside the coral, forming a mass of thread-like interconnecting tunnels. A substantial part of each sponge colony is buried in the coral skeleton but sponges still need a connection to the surface in order to be able to draw in water for feeding and respiration. *Cliona delitrix* occurs throughout the region, on shallow to deep reefs.

16 VARIABLE BORING SPONGE
Siphonodictyon coralliphagum

Siphonodictyon coralliphagum usually appears as a cluster of yellow chimneys, fingers or tubes protruding from the coral surface. Sometimes it forms encrustations. From the outside, it does not look as though this sponge is causing much damage, but it actually excavates large holes within the coral. Like other boring sponges it plays an important ecological role because it severely weakens corals and may cause their collapse. This species is particularly common in the Caribbean, generally occurring at depths below about 10m (33ft)

CNIDARIANS

Members of this group (phylum) are well represented on the reef. Not only does it include the reef building hard corals, but also sea fans, sea whips, anemones, black corals, jellyfish and many other forms. At first glance these animals might seem very different from each other, but they have a number of features in common.

Within the group there are two basic body forms – the attached polyp and the floating medusa. The typical polyp is anemone-like, consisting of a tube closed at the attached end and with a mouth and ring of tentacles at the other. Food is captured by the tentacles and passed through the mouth into the internal cavity where it is digested. Wastes exit through the mouth. The medusa is bell-shaped with a central mouth and usually with tentacles around the perimeter.

A feature of cnidarians is that they are armed with stinging cells that are fired off for capture of prey and also for defence. These cnidae (nematocysts) are too small to be seen with the naked eye, but their effect can be felt on human skin. Cnidarians reproduce sexually, producing floating larvae (planula) that colonize new areas. In most species within the group, polyps split or bud to produce new polyps, which remain attached, so forming a colony. A large coral colony may consist of thousands of polyps, all of which originate from the settlement of a single planula.

HYDROIDS

Most hydroids have a complicated life history. The main stage is the polyp, which is attached and forms delicate fern-like growths. During sexual reproduction many hydroids produce a small, short-lived jellyfish called a hydromedusa. Hydroids have tiny polyps, but many of them have a powerful sting.

1 FEATHER PLUME HYDROID
Aglaophenia latecarinata

Aglaophenia latecarinata is one of several species of small, feathery hydroid that occurs at all depths in the Florida region. It grows to a height of about 7cm (2¾in) and usually occurs as a cluster of fine stems, which have alternately arranged branches along their length. Tiny white polyps are just visible, lining the branches.

15 Red Boring Sponge

16 Variable Boring Sponge

Example of a Cnidarian – open and closed coral polyp

1 Feather Plume Hydroid

2 CLUB HYDROMEDUSA

Orchistoma pileus

The medusa is the dominant phase in this species, rather than the polyp. It is only about 2.5cm (1in) in diameter, but sometimes occurs in large aggregations close to the surface of the water. The dome is transparent with long, fine tentacles trailing from its perimeter. There is a whitish, club-shaped swelling at the base of each tentacle, where it joins the bell. Hydromedusae can be distinguished from true jellyfish by examining the margin of the bell, which turns inwards, forming a 'lip' known as the velum.

HYDROCORALS

Hydrocorals are calcified hydroids. Their outer surface is smooth and pin-head sized pores that house the polyps are just visible. There are two types of polyp: the dactylozooid for defence, and the gastrozooid for feeding.

1 BRANCHING FIRE CORAL

Millepora alcicornis

The dactylozooids of fire corals have long, hair-like tentacles. If examined under a microscope, batteries of stinging cells (nematocysts or cnidae) are visible. This heavy armoury inflicts a painful sting. The dactylozooids surround much shorter, stouter polyps, which have a mouth and are responsible for capturing and ingesting prey. *M. alciornis* is one of three species of calcified hydroid that occur in the region. The other two species have solid plates or blades and are important reef builders. *Millepora alcicornis* has a much less robust growth form, but even so, contributes to reef building. It often encrusts and grows over gorgonians, taking their shape, or else forms branching colonies. It is common throughout the region, from shallow to deep water.

2 ROSE LACE CORAL

Stylaster roseus

Unlike firecorals, the dactylozooids of stylastid corals lack tentacles and so do not have a hairy appearance. The rose lace coral is a very beautiful, calcified hydroid that grows only to a height of about 10cm (4in). It is very delicate, with fine, tapering branches. Its colour ranges from purple to pink, and the branch ends are paler. Polyps are situated in tiny cups that can just be made out, scattered over the branches. Rose lace coral is common throughout the region, but is restricted to sheltered, shaded habitats such as underhangs and crevices.

GORGONIANS

Gorgonians are represented only by the polyp and do not have a medusoid phase in the life cycle. They belong to a group called the octocorallia in which, as the name implies, the polyps have eight tentacles. These tentacles are branched, giving them a feathery appearance. Gorgonians such as sea whips, fans and plumes are abundant on reefs in the western Atlantic and are often mistakenly referred to as soft corals. True soft corals also have eight feathery tentacles, but lack the rod-like central core and fused spicules that give the gorgonians their strong, flexible stems. In contrast to the Indo-Pacific, soft corals are very rarely seen in the western Atlantic, and are restricted to deep water.

1 ENCRUSTING GORGONIAN

Erythropodium caribaeorium

When the polyps are contracted, *Erythropodium caribaeorium* appears as a reddish-brown, smooth mat, dotted with tiny, usually white-rimmed pores. When the polyps are extended the mat takes on a soft 'hairy' appearance. This encrusting gorgonian occurs in most reef habitats throughout the area and may form colonies up to 1m (3ft 3in) across.

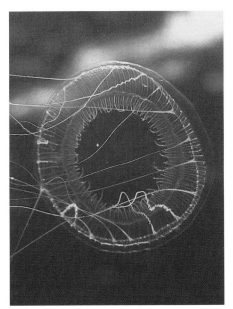

2 Club Hydromedusa

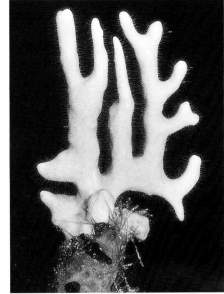

1 Branching Fire Coral

2 Rose Lace Coral

1 Encrusting Gorgonian

2 BLACK SEA ROD

Plexaura homomalla

The black sea rod forms bushy colonies up to 60cm (2ft) tall. It has a darkish stem and paler yellow-brown polyps and, if damaged, releases a brown pigment into the water. This is a potent irritant but is of great interest to pharmacologists because of its bioactivity. It has been found to contain prostanoids in concentrations ten million times higher than that of other animals. Initially, *Plexaura* was harvested for analysis, in order that work could be carried out to convert the prostanoids to biochemically active prostaglandins (used to treat cardiovascular disease, asthma and gastric ulcers). Within a year, synthetic production was perfected and harvesting ceased. *P. homomalla* is common throughout the region and is found on seaward reefs at all depths.

3 GIANT SLIT-PORE SEA ROD

Plexaurella nutans

Plexaurella nutans has thick, brownish or grey stems up to about 1.4m (4ft 6in) tall that generally branch only once. The polyps retract into slit-like pores, which have a slightly raised lip. This species occurs throughout the region, on seaward reefs at depths of 10 to 50m (33 to 165ft). A number of other *Plexaurella* species occur in the area. These are difficult to distinguish from each other, but differ from *P. nutans* in being shorter and branching more frequently.

4 SEA PLUME

Pseudopterogorgia spp.

Sea plumes typically form tall, branching plumes, with some individual bushes over 2m (6ft 7in) tall. There are about twelve species of *Pseudopterogorgia* in the region, most of which are impossible to distinguish from one another underwater. The polyps are generally arranged in rows, and the pores from which they protrude are flush with the surface. In shallow, wave-sheltered situations sea plumes may flourish to such an extent that they form dense thickets.

5 COMMON SEA FAN

Gorgonia ventalina

Sea fans have strong, flexible stems that branch profusely, usually in one plane, to form a delicate meshwork. They prefer situations with some water movement, and align themselves at right angles to the current flow in order to maximize the chances of planktonic food passing close to the polyps. The common sea fan grows to a maximum height of about 2m (6ft 7in) and is usually purple in colour although it may appear greyish-brown when the polyps are extended. It is common throughout the region, particularly in shallow water down to depths of 15m (49ft).

6 VENUS SEA FAN

Gorgonia flabellum

The venus sea fan is similar to *G. ventalina*, although it seldom grows to such a large size; its maximum height is generally about 1m (3ft 3in). It is yellowish-green in colour and sometimes has short branches protruding at right angles to the main fan. Another difference is that the branches are slightly flattened at right angles to the plane of the main fan, while in *G. ventalina* they are rounded or slightly flattened in the same plane as the fan. The venus sea fan prefers shallow water with plenty of water movement, and it is not unusual for it to be exposed in very low tides. It is found throughout the region and is especially common in the Bahamas and Caribbean.

7 DEEPWATER SEA FAN

Iciligorgia schrammi

The deepwater sea fan does not occur in water shallower than 10m (33ft), is usually seen below 20m (66ft) and has been found to depths of over 360m (1,180ft). Like the shallow water forms, the branches spread out in a single plane. They are flattened in the same plane as the fan, and the polyps are arranged in rows down each of the narrow edges. It is usually dark brown in colour and may be well over 1.25m (4ft) in height. It is found throughout the region and is especially abundant on steep slopes and walls (including canyons) where there is some current.

2 Black Sea Rod

3 Giant Split-pore Sea Rod

4 Sea Plume

5 Common Sea Fan

6 Venus Sea Fan

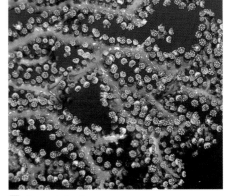

7 Deepwater Sea Fan

8 DEVIL'S SEA WHIP
Ellisella barbadensis
The genus *Ellisella* is widespread in the Caribbean, forming unbranched or sparsely branched stems that are long and stiff, yet flexible. Some species occur in clumps, but *E. barbadensis* grows as a single stem. It can reach a length of 2.5m (8ft 3in) and is orange-red in colour with white polyps that are usually extended during the day. Unlike hard corals, it does not have zooxanthellae in its tissues and so relies entirely on catching planktonic prey. Sea whips like other cnidarians, reproduce sexually by producing sperm and eggs. These fuse to form a free-swimming larva which settle on the reef after a few weeks. *E. barbadensis* can also reproduce asexually by pinching a small piece off the top. The tissue degenerates along a small portion of the whip until only the central, horny rod remains. This then gets broken off by water movement, drops on to the reef surface, cements and grows. *E. barbadensis* is seen occasionally throughout the region, especially on walls and steep outer reefs below about 20m (66ft) in depth.

HEXACORALLIA

This subdivision of the anthozoans contains anemones, zoanthids, corallimorphs and hard corals. They are called hexacorallia because the polyp tentacles are arranged in multiples of six (rather than eight as in the gorgonians).

ANEMONES

1 GIANT ANEMONE
Condylactis gigantea
C. gigantea is the only Caribbean anemone that grows reasonably large, up to 30cm (12in). The column is usually hidden, but the long, pale tentacles with slightly bulbous, usually pinkish tips, are unmistakable. Over 30 species of reef fish are known to associate with it, mostly to avoid predators. Typically, they swim carefully to avoid touching the anemone, but nine species (mostly blennies) have behavioural and physiological adaptations for living unharmed among the stinging tentacles. Even so, the association is not obligatory (as it is in the Indo-Pacific anemonefish). Anemone shrimps (*Thor* species, with short antennae), cleaner shrimps (*Periclimenes* species, with very long antennae) and small crabs may also hide among the tentacles. Although by no means speedy, this anemene can creep along on its basal disk to find the most suitable position on the reef. It is common throughout the region, occurring in most habitats.

2 CORKSCREW ANEMONE
Bartholomea annulata
The corkscrew anemone has transparent tentacles up to 10cm (4in) long, with white rings arranged in spirals. These are batteries of stinging cells (nematocysts), which give a mild sting if accidentally touched. The column of *Bartholomea* is buried in sand and rubble, or hidden in recesses, and the tentacles retract very rapidly if the animal is disturbed. Red snapping shrimps (*Alpheus armatus*) and Pederson cleaner shrimps (*Periclimenes pedersoni*) are often associated with this species. It is common throughout the region, occurring in both sand and coral habitats in shallow and deep water.

3 BRANCHING ANEMONE
Lebrunia danae
The anemone has its column buried in crevices, with only the tentacles visible. These are of two kinds. Around the margin of the oral disk is a ring of long, tapering tentacles that are extended mainly at night, when the animal is feeding. During the day, usually all that can be seen is a mass of 'false' tentacles (pseudotentacles) that are shorter and have branched ends. These are brown in colour and covered with whitish bumps that are packed with nematocysts, and can give a noticeable sting. When spread out, the pseudotentacles may be as much as 30cm (12in) across. *L. danae* occurs throughout the region in most reef areas.

8 Devil's Sea Whip

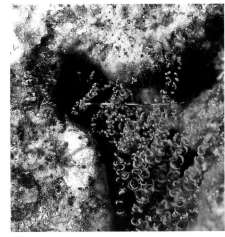

2 Corkscrew Anemone

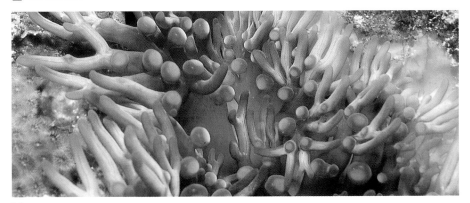

1 Giant Anemone

3 Branching Anemone

ZOANTHIDS

Zoanthids are small, anemone-like cnidarians that may be solitary or colonial. They have two cycles of tentacles arranged in close-set rings around the margin of the oral disk.

1 HYDROID ZOANTHID
Parazoanthus tunicans
This zoanthid encrusts the branches of the feather bush hydroid *Dentitheca dendritica*. The individual zoanthid polyps are about 0.5cm (¼in) across and have numerous thin tentacles, which are orange or brownish in colour. The zoanthids themselves do not sting but the hydroid does. *P. tunicans* occurs throughout the region, with its host hydroid, which prefers reef areas with some current.

2 GOLDEN ZOANTHID
Parazoanthus swiftii
The golden zoanthid has a symbiotic relationship with several species of sponge, and may cover a significant amount of their surface. It is particularly common on the green finger sponge *Lotrochota birotulata*, forming long rows that wind around the branches. Individual polyps are about 0.5cm (¼in) in diameter. The golden zoanthid is toxic to fish, and its presence probably discourages sponge-eating fish from launching an attack. The brilliant golden-yellow colour of the polyps and tentacles may act as a warning to fish to steer clear. This species is common in the Caribbean and Bahamas, occurring in most reef habitats.

3 MAT ZOANTHID
Zoanthus pulchellus
As its name implies, this zoanthid forms a dense mat of closely packed individuals. The polyps are about 1cm (½in) in diameter, and are connected at the base. They are greenish in colour and each has two rings of very short tentacles around the perimeter of the disk. The mat zoanthid is common in the Caribbean and Bahamas, especially on shallow reef tops.

CORALLIMORPHARIANS

Corallimorpharians can be mistaken for other types of anemone, but are usually distinguished by the fairly flat oral disk, small protruding mouth and short tentacles that radiate out from their centre like the spokes of a wheel.

1 FLORIDA CORALLIMORPH
Ricordea florida
Individual polyps in this species are up to about 5cm (2in) in diameter and are usually packed closely together. Extremely short, stubby tentacles cover the oral disk. These are usually greenish, often with mouth and outer rows of tentacles a different shade from the rest. *Ricordea florida* is found throughout the region and may form extensive carpets over reef limestone in shallow water.

2 ORANGE BALL CORALLIMORPH
Pseudocorynactis caribbeorum
This beautiful and very distinctive coral-limorph is seen only at night, when the tentacles are extended to catch zooplankton. The column is bedded into a crevice or sand and the entire animal disappears from view if disturbed. Unusually for a corallimorph, the tentacles in this species are quite long, up to 5cm (2in). They are nearly transparent with orange tips, and the column is also orange. The orange ball corallimorph is found on reefs and sandy habitats in the Caribbean, but is not common.

1 Hydroid Zoanthid

2 Golden Zoanthid

3 Mat Zoanthid

1 Florida Corallimmorph

2 Orange Ball Corallimorph

SCLERACTINIAN CORALS

The polyps of scleractinian (also known as 'hard' or 'stony') corals are similar to those of anemones, with tentacles arranged in multiples of six. They differ because each polyp produces a cup-like calcium carbonate skeleton (the corallite) in which it sits. Most stony corals are colonial, with hundreds or thousands of corallites joined together to form a solid structure called the corallum. Corals capture food using stinging cells (nematocysts), but also obtain some of their nutrition from thousands of single-celled plants (zooxanthellae) that live in their tissues and are a vital part of their make-up. Like all plants, the zooxanthellae manufacture organic matter from carbon dioxide and sunlight. Some of this material is passed on to their hosts. Zooxanthellae need to be in a well-lit location to function properly, and this is one of the main reasons why corals compete for space on the shallow reef. Corals fight for space in a number of ways, and some are more aggressive than others. They may simply overgrow or shade each other, but they also use chemical warfare. Some develop special 'sweeper' tentacles that have an extra long reach and are usually employed at night. Others have internal threads (mesenteric filaments), which are extruded and actually digest neighbouring coral tissue. The result of all this is a whitish, dead band that separates adjacent coral colonies.

Scleractinian corals are relatively easy to identify as a group, but occasionally are mistaken for 'rock' or confused with other reef dwellers that produce a calcium carbonate skeleton – such as fire coral and some of the red algae. Scleractinian corals have distinct patterns on the outside that relate to the underlying skeleton and the arrangement of the coral polyps – they are never smooth or featureless. Identifying hard corals to species can be difficult. Identification relies heavily on skeletal characteristics, and coral skeletons have a complex structure in which only the outer part is visible. Often the fine detail is obscured by a covering of living tissue. However, using a combination of features, including growth form, it is possible to identify positively some of the 70 or so species that occur in the Caribbean.

CORAL BLEACHING

Under stressful conditions, corals lose their pigmented zooxanthellae, turn white and begin to starve. They can survive for weeks or even months like this, but their health deteriorates and they die unless the stress factor is removed.

What are these stresses? The first serious occurrence of 'coral bleaching' in the western Atlantic was in Bermuda in 1987 and 1988, and coincided with the longest period of elevated sea temperature in Bermuda for 38 years. In 1990, bleaching was severe all across the Caribbean, again coinciding with hot sea temperatures (the highest ever recorded). In 1998 further bleaching occurred as sea surface temperatures hit an all-time high. Other factors such as ultraviolet radiation may also be implicated in bleaching, but elevated temperature is the main problem. Despite being tropical organisms, corals have a fairly narrow temperature tolerance. With a few exceptions, they flourish within the range 25 to 29 °C, but bleach when the temperature is held above that for a few weeks by only one or two degrees.

BLACK BAND DISEASE

It was not until the late 1970s that scientists began to report the occurrence of diseases in corals. Whether or not these ailments had been around before then and simply gone unnoticed is not known, but there is concern that as reefs become more stressed, so they become more susceptible to disease – just like humans. Black band disease starts as a small dot, which then spreads in ring-like fashion across the coral colony. The organism primarily responsible is a filamentous blue-green alga (the cyanobacterium *Phormidium corallyticum*), but a complex disease community soon develops, manifesting itself as a conspicuous dark line. This line may progress daily over the colony by as much as 1cm (½in). It leaves bare skeleton behind, which rapidly becomes colonized by algae and other organisms. An identical disease has also been found on a number of gorgonians in the Caribbean (such as *Gorgonia*, *Plexaura* and *Pseudopterogorgia*) but not on Indo-Pacific species.

1 Coral Bleaching

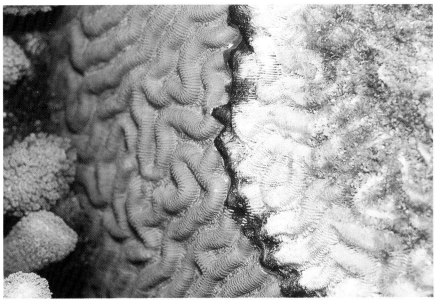

2 Black Band Desease

ACROPORIDAE

Corals of the genus *Acropora* often dominate in shallow areas, and are important reef builders with a long geological history. Stands of *Acropora* on some reefs in the western Atlantic have been quite badly hit by bleaching, disease and storms, but recovery may be reasonably fast if conditions are suitable. *Acropora* species are amongst the fastest growing of all corals, with the staghorn varieties adding as much as 15cm a year in branch length. The identification of *Acropora* species is much easier in the western Atlantic than in the Indo-Pacific, with three species in the former and over a hundred in the latter. The three western Atlantic species have different habitat preferences and typically occur in well-defined zones. All *Acropora* species have small, separate corallites, and polyps that are normally retracted during the day.

1 ELKHORN CORAL

Acropora palmata
This important and widespread coral usually forms thick, stout branches that are flattened horizontally and aligned to face the swell. It prefers shallow water exposed to continual wave action, and is common down to depths of about 10m (33ft), but may occur as deep as 16m (52ft). If broken or overturned in storms it is capable of re-cementing and continuing to grow. In situations exposed to extremely heavy surf, it may be totally encrusting, illustrating the highly adaptable nature of corals and their responses to the environment in which they live.

2 STAGHORN CORAL

Acropora cervicornis
The branches in this species are much more slender than in *A. palmata*, and do not arise from a substantial base. It is less resistant to wave action than elkhorn coral and occurs at more sheltered sites or in slightly deeper water – sometimes as deep as 40m (130ft) or more. It has one of the most rapid growth rates of all western Atlantic corals – adding up to 15cm

(6in) in branch length annually under ideal conditions. Extensive stands of staghorn coral may be present on shallow reefs where wave action is not too strong. In deeper water, around 20m (66ft) or more, or on more wave-exposed reefs, *A. cervicornis* may form large mounds as much as 5m (16ft 5in) tall, known as haystack reefs, separated by sandy channels tens of metres wide. There is a third species (*A. prolifera*) with thinner branches that may form small plate-like colonies and is known as fused staghorn.

AGARICIIDAE

1 GRAHAM'S SHEET CORAL

Agaricia grahamae
Members of the family *Agariciidae* are well represented in the western Atlantic, occurring from shallow water to depths of 80m (260ft) or more. Most colonies are foliaceous or encrusting and they often have vertical crests or fronds. Colonies of *A. grahamae* may be as much as 2m (6ft 7in) in diameter. Corallites are small, crowded and have joined walls. Polyp mouths appear as minute pin-sized centres. There are probably seven species of *Agaricia* in the western Atlantic but identification is not particularly easy as there are overlaps between species.

PORITIDAE

1 FINGER CORAL

Porites porites
Corals belonging to the genus *Porites* have pin-head sized corallites with joined walls that give the appearance of a miniature honeycomb. Several species occur in the region, and growth forms include crusts, mounds and branching colonies. *Porites porites* is one of the commonest species, occurring widely in many reef habitats from shallow back reefs to depths of 50m (165ft). Colonies may be over 1m (3ft 3in) in diameter, and branches may be stout or elongate, widely spaced or crowded, according to the environmental conditions. Polyps are usually extended during the day, giving the coral a fuzzy appearance.

1 Elkhorn Coral

2 Staghorn Coral

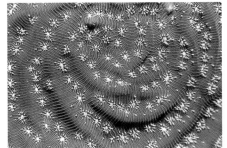

1 Graham's Sheet Coral

1 Finger Coral

FAVIIDAE

Faviid corals are well represented on Caribbean reefs, with seven genera and about a dozen species. Colonies range from massive domes several metres in diameter to inconspicuous fist-sized growths. Corallites are separate in some species, but in others are joined to form long valleys.

1 TUBE CORAL

Cladocora arbuscula

Cladocera is distinguished from other faviids by its growth form. It forms smallish clumps less than 15cm (6in) in diameter in which the corallites arise from an encrusting base and may branch. Each branch represents a single corallite and these are narrow, approximately 2.5mm (1/10in), but elongate, up to 8mm (1/3in). Tube coral is found in sandy, turbid areas such as seagrass beds and often much of the colony is covered with sediment. It occurs down to depths of 20m (66ft); there is a second species (*C. debilis*) that is found on deep, clear water reefs, generally below 24m (79ft).

2 BOULDER STAR CORAL

Montastraea annularis

Montastraea annularis is one of the most important reef building corals in the Caribbean, forming massive colonies that are usually lobed or rounded in shallow water and flattened or plate-like on deep reefs. *M. annularis* is found in most reef habitats, from depths of about 2m (6ft 7in) to 40m (130ft) and is often the dominant coral at mid-depth of 7 to 22m (23 to 72ft). It is distinguished by the rounded, crowded corallites that seldom exceed 3mm (1/10in) in diameter.

3 GREAT STAR CORAL

Montastraea cavernosa

M. cavernosa is readily identified by the large, approximately10mm (1/3in), slightly protuberant corallites. Like *M. annularis* it is an important reef builder that is very common in a range of habitats and may be dominant at depths of 12 to 30m (39 to 98ft). With increasing depth the domes change first to low helmet-shaped colonies, then to plates or sheets, which are increasingly porous. Many corals are hermaphrodites, but this species is one that has either male or female colonies – but there is nothing to show this from the outside!

4 GROOVED BRAIN CORAL

Diploria labyrinthiformis

Diploria species are usually massive and rounded but may be flattened or encrusting. The corallites are united in longitudinal series and their fused walls form ridges across the surface of the colony. Polyp mouths are visible in the valleys as rounded or slit-like apertures. Of the three species that occur in the area, *D. labyrinthiformis* is distinctive because there is always a groove along the top of the wall. It is a fairly common coral, especially on seaward reef slopes from depths of 5 to 15m (16 to 165ft).

MEANDRINIDAE

1 PILLAR CORAL

Dendrogyra cylindrus

Dendrogyra cylindrus is a striking coral that occurs sporadically on shallow reefs throughout the region. Colonies may be over 3m (9ft 10in) tall, and consist of a columnar base from which arise upwardly pointing spires. The surface of the coral is covered by a mass of pale brown tentacles that are about 5mm (1/6in) long and retract rapidly when touched. Polyps are mostly joined in longitudinal series to form narrow valleys with wide walls.

MUSSIDAE

Members of the family *Mussidae* have large corallites, strong spines on the surface and a rather fleshy appearance. Polyps are retracted during the day.

1 SOLITARY DISK CORAL

Scolymia wellsi

Scolymia is a solitary mussid with a disk-like corallum. There are three species that are not easy to distinguish underwater. *S. wellsi* is the smallest, with a disk up to about 7cm (2 3/4in) diameter. It is usually darkish green or brown in colour and is seen occasionally on steep, deep reefs throughout the region.

1 Tube Coral

2 Boulder Star Coral

3 Great Star Coral

4 Grooved Brain Coral

1 Pillar Coral

1 Solitary Disc Coral

2 RIDGED CACTUS CORAL

Mycetophyllia lamarckiana
There are five species of *Mycetophyllia* in the region. *M. lamarckiana* may occur as a flattened plate, or a crust with broad, leafy margins, and is up to 30cm (12in) in diameter. The outer margin is raised, and ridges run from the outside towards the centre without a break but do not meet in the middle (*M. danaana* is similar but the ridges have breaks in them and usually run across the centre.) The living tissue is green, bluish or brownish in colour. It forms a fleshy covering over the skeleton, but the long spines typical of this family are still visible underneath. This coral is seen occasionally on reefs throughout the region, especially below 12m (40ft) on steep slopes and ledges.

DENDROPHYLLIIDAE

1 ORANGE CUP CORAL

Tubastraea coccinea
This coral forms clumps up to about 30cm (12in) in diameter. The corallites are about 1.5cm (⅝in) wide and have bright orange polyps that are usually extended only at night. Dendrophylliids lack symbiotic algae and so are entirely reliant on plankton for their food.

The fate of small animals lured close by the beam of a torch at night can be seen as they are rapidly captured and passed to the mouth. Although *T. coccinea* is typical of the deep reef, it is shade rather than depth that determines its distribution. Where drop-offs and undercut surfaces occur in shallow water it competes successfully with shallow water corals. It is absent from Florida but occurs elsewhere in the region, sometimes in abundance if conditions are suitable.

ANTIPATHARIA

Antipatharians (black corals), are found in shallow water where there are steep faces, but are more typical of deep reefs and occur widely throughout the region. There are many types of black coral. Some are very small and delicate with a highly divided, tangled mass of fine branches. In contrast, on vertical faces (especially where there is a current) there may be enormous bushes, several metres tall and hundreds of years old. There are also whip-like black corals that resemble the gorgonian whips mentioned in the previous section but have a stem that is coiled like a loose spring and polyp tentacles that are unbranched.

JELLYFISH

'True' jellyfish (scyphozoa) spend all their time afloat, as medusae. The bell varies greatly in shape and size, as does the number and length of tentacles that occur around its margin. The mouth is at the end of a tube that often has frilly 'oral lobes' around it. Jellyfish can swim by pulsating the bell, but they are largely at the mercy of ocean currents, and often get washed ashore in large numbers.

1 MOON JELLY

Aurelia aurita
The moon jelly is easily recognized by its bluish-transparent bell and the white reproductive organs that are in the outline shape of a four-leafed clover. It has numerous short tentacles around the rim of the bell, which is up to 25cm (9¾in) in diameter. Its sting is very mild, generally producing little more than a momentary tingling sensation. It is common throughout the region.

2 SEA THIMBLE

Linuche unguiculata
The sea thimble gets its name from the shape of the bell, which is relatively deep and narrow. It is brownish in colour and has widely spaced, short tentacles around the margin. Its sting is mild, except on sensitive skins. It occurs in warm waters around the globe but may be overlooked because of its small size – less than 2cm (¾in) in diameter.

2 Ringed Cactus Coral

Orange Cup Coral

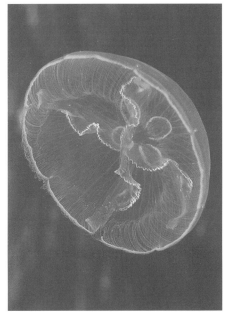

1 Moon Jellyfish

2 Sea Thimble

3 MANGROVE UPSIDEDOWN JELLY

Cassiopea xamachana

Upsidedown jellyfish have a saucer-shaped bell up to 15cm (6in) in diameter, and oral arms that branch into thousands of tiny frills. These are packed with microscopic unicellular algae (zooxanthellae) and the jellyfish gains much of its nutrition from this symbiotic relationship. It is for this reason that the jellyfish rests on the bottom, 'sunbathing' upside down in order to expose the algae to maximum light. When on the move they swim in the normal way, with the bell uppermost and the tentacles beneath. There are two common species of upsidedown jellyfish in the region. *C. xamachana* has longer oral arms than *C. frondosa*, the upsidedown jelly, and is usually greyish rather than brown. Both have a mild sting.

WORMS

Many types of worm live on and around coral reefs, but most are small or hidden from view and seldom noticed by divers. Those most frequently encountered are flatworms and various types of segmented (polychaete) worms.

FLATWORMS – PLATYHELMINTHES

1 LEOPARD FLATWORM

Pseudoceros pardalis

Flatworms have leaf-like bodies and glide along the seabed using numerous tiny cilia that beat rhythmically on their underside. *Pseudoceros pardalis* is one of the largest of the many species of flatworm that occur in the area, and has muscles as well as cilia to help it move. The rippling effect of muscular waves passing along the body can be seen when it occasionally takes off and swims in open water. Like other flatworms, *P. pardalis* is a carnivore, feeding on smaller worms and invertebrates. The mouth is on the underside and the head end has simple eyes and two short antennae. It reaches a length of about 5cm (2in) and is seen occasionally on reefs throughout the region.

POLYCHAETE WORMS

Polychaete worms (bristleworms and tubeworms) belong in the Phylum Annelida. This large group also includes earthworms and leeches, but it is the polychaetes that are so abundant in the marine environment. Most of the species seen by divers are those that live in tubes attached to the seabed. The free-living ones tend to be secretive and hidden from view.

1 MAGNIFICENT FEATHER DUSTER

Sabellastarte magnifica

This polychaete lives in a soft tube that it manufactures for itself. The body of the worm is hidden and protected by the tube, which is buried in sand or tucked into a crevice. All that is usually visible is the top end of the tube and the head end of the worm with its two whorls of brown and white tentacles (radioles). These are up to 10cm (4in) in diameter, and retract rapidly if the animal is disturbed. Cilia on the radioles create water currents and help filter food particles from the water. *S. magnifica* occurs throughout the region in a range of habitats to a depth of about 20m (66ft).

2 SOCIAL FEATHER DUSTER

Bispira brunnea

B. brunnea also lives in a soft tube. It is easily distinguished from other species because it grows in clusters, and the tube is usually free for much of its length. The crown of radioles is up to about 3cm (1¼in) in diameter and may be white, lavender or brown in colour, depending partly on geographic location. This species is common in the Bahamas and Caribbean, occurring from shallow water down to depths of about 20m (66ft).

3 Mangrove Upsidedown Jelly

1 Leopard Flatworm

1 Magnificent Feather Duster

2 Social Feather Duster

3 SPLIT-CROWN FEATHER DUSTER
Anamobaea orstedii
This species can be recognized by the crown of radioles that is up to 5cm (2in) in diameter, oval in shape and split into two identical halves. It lives in a soft tube that is normally concealed inside coral limestone. Like other fanworms, the head end has sensory eye spots and the animal retracts immediately if a shadow passes over it. This species is common throughout the region, occurring from shallow water down to depths of about 23m (75ft).

4 CHRISTMAS TREE WORM
Spirobranchus giganteus
The Christmas tree worm occurs throughout the tropics. It has brightly coloured tentacles (red, blue, purple, yellow or green) that protrude from the coral surface as two fan-shaped spiral whorls. When the tentacles are withdrawn, the calcareous tube can be plugged with a small plate. This species prefers living coral, especially massive species. Following a short planktonic stage, the larvae settle on live coral, probably finding an entry point where a polyp has died or been damaged. They do not actively burrow, but avoid being engulfed by continually adding new tube as the coral grows.

5 STAR HORSESHOE WORM
Pomatostegus stellatus
P. stellatus is another species with a calcareous tube, but this is normally hidden from view by the horseshoe-shaped crown of tentacles that may be nearly 4cm (1 ½in) in diameter. The radioles are usually red with yellow tips, occasionally yellow, orange or brownish. This species lives on coral heads and grows in a similar way to the Christmas tree worm. It is very common on reefs throughout the region, occurring from shallow water to depths of over 30m (98ft).

6 BEARDED FIREWORM
Hermodice carunculata
The bearded fireworm is a free-living species and spends much of its time out in the open. It is up to 30cm (12in) in length, brightly coloured and has clusters of white bristles along its sides. These are filled with venom and cause intense irritation if they break off in the skin. This species preys on over ten species of hard coral. It also feeds on anemones, gorgonians and zoanthids. Branch tips of corals are attacked, causing lesions several centimetres in diameter. Where fireworm predation is heavy, significant damage may be done. The fireworm occurs throughout the region.

MOLLUSCS

Molluscs are a diverse group containing thousands of species. They have a number of features in common, including (in most species) an external, calcareous shell, a soft body with a covering called the mantle, a muscular foot, a tongue-like radula for feeding, and gills for respiration. Of the six main groups of mollusc, only three are common on reefs – the gastropods, bivalves and cephalopods.

GASTROPODS

Gastropods include snails with a spiral shell (prosobranchs) and those that either have a reduced shell or no shell at all (opisthobranchs).

1 QUEEN CONCH
Strombus gigas
This is the largest of the six species of conch that occur in the region, growing to a maximum length of about 30cm (12in). Like all conch, the shell has a notch on its lip through which the stalked right eye of the animal normally protrudes. The inside of the shell is a beautiful pink colour. Queen conch browse on algae and detritus on the surface of sand or rubble and are expert at digging, manoeuvring and defending themselves using the long, claw-like horny operculum on the foot. *S. gigas* occurs on seagrass beds and sandy habitats throughout the region, from shallow water to depths of over 30m (98ft).

3 Split-crown Feather Duster

4 Christmas Tree Worm

5 Star Horseshoe Worm

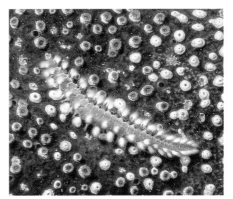

6 Bearded Fireworm

1 Queen Conch

2 ATLANTIC GRAY COWRIE
Cypraea cinerea
Cowries have smooth, often brightly coloured, shells and are amongst the best known of all the gastropod molluscs, widely used for decoration and even as a form of money in the past. The shell is kept clean and free of marine growths by the mantle of living tissue which can be extended over it. The slit-like aperture on what appears to be the underside of the shell is actually produced as a result of the main shell whorl growing over and covering the central spire. *C. cinerea* is one of many species of cowrie that occurs on and around reefs in the region. It tends to hide under ledges and among corals during the day, emerging at night in search of food. It is mottled brown in colour, and its maximum size is about 2.5cm (1in).

3 FLAMINGO TONGUE
Cyphoma gibbosum
The flamingo tongue is about 2.5cm (1in) long, and living specimens are easily recognized by the creamy mantle with its black-rimmed orange spots. If the animal is disturbed the mantle is retracted, exposing the smooth, pinkish shell beneath. The flamingo tongue lives and feeds on sea fans and gorgonian whips, stripping away the living tissue to leave bare stem behind. It is common on reefs throughout the region, from shallow water to depths of about 14m (46ft).

4 FINGERPRINT CYPHOMA
Cyphoma signatum
The mantle of the fingerprint cyphoma is beautifully patterned in gold and black, and is usually extended to cover the creamish-coloured shell completely. This species also feeds on gorgonians, and occurs in the same habitats as *C. gibbosum* but is much less common. It has a narrow shell that grows to about 2.5cm (1in) in length.

5 LETTUCE SEA SLUG
Tridachia crispata
The lettuce sea slug *Tridachia crispata* is a sacoglossan. It resembles 'true' sea-slugs (nudibranchs) but lacks exposed gills, and differs in feeding exclusively on plants. It does this by piercing the cell walls with its radula teeth and sucking out the contents, including the chloroplasts. These are kept intact and relocated on the slug's back, where they continue to photosynthesize, producing organic material that the slug can use. The frills on the back also contain poison glands, which help to ward off predators. The lettuce sea slug is common on reefs throughout the region, from shallow water to depths of about 12m (39ft).

6 WHITE-SPECKLED NUDIBRANCH
Paleo jubatus
Like all nudibranchs, *P. jubatus* lacks any vestige of a shell. The head end has sensory tentacles and there are often feathery gills and sometimes fleshy projections (cerata) on the upper side. The latter are numerous in the white-speckled nudibranch. A creeping foot is beneath. These molluscs are exclusively carnivorous, and are quite likely to be eating whatever they are found sitting on – such as sponges or hydroids. *P. jubatus* feeds on gorgonians of the genus *Plexaurella*, and is found occasionally in the Caribbean from shallow water to depths of about 30m (98ft). Most nudibranchs are unpalatable and the bright orange colour of this species may act as a warning to predators to leave them alone.

7 LEATHER-BACKED DORIS
Platydoris angustipes
This species is red in colour, to match the encrusting sponges on which it feeds. Tentacles are present at the head end and there is a cluster of gills at the back but, like other dorids, this species lacks cerata. It is seen occasionally on shallow reefs of the Bahamas and the Caribbean. Its maximum size is about 10cm (4in). This species, like other sea slugs, is hermaphrodite and produces planktonic larvae. The life span of nudibranchs is usually only a year or two, but during this time they may reproduce many times.

2 Atlantic Gray Cowrie

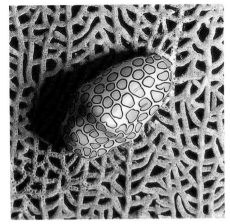

3 Flamingo Tongue

4 Fingerprint Cyphoma

5 Lettuce Sea Slug

6 White-speckled Nudibranch

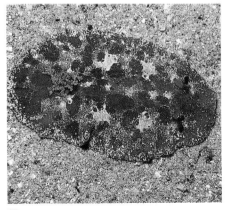

7 Leather-backed Doris

BIVALVES

1 ROUGH FILECLAM

Lima scabra

Bivalves have a soft body enclosed within two hinged shell valves. *Lima scabra* is the largest of three *Lima* species that occur in the area. It lives in crevices and usually all that is visible is the edge of the bright orange mantle with its long tentacles and internal fringe. These extensions of the mantle may also be orange, but tend to be white in specimens from deeper water. It grows to about 7.5cm (3in) in length and is common on reefs throughout the region from shallow water to depths of 40m (130ft).

CEPHALOPODS

Cephalopods are the most advanced of all the molluscs. They are intelligent animals with well-developed eyes and complex behaviour patterns. The shell has either been lost or is reduced and internal. Tentacles extend from the head and perform a variety of functions.

1 CARIBBEAN REEF SQUID

Sepioteuthis sepioidea

Squid have ten arms with suction disks on their inner surface. They are expert swimmers adapted for life in open water. *Sepioteuthis sepioidea* is the only squid normally seen on Caribbean reefs. During the day it usually aggregates in small groups and hovers above the reef, jetting away if disturbed, sometimes leaving behind a cloud of ink. At night it tends to be confused by torchlight and can be approached more closely. It feeds on small fish. The arms in the species are quite short and colour is variable according to mood and habitat. Like all squid, this species has a short life span of about one year. During that time it reaches a length of about 30cm (12in).

2 CARIBBEAN REEF OCTOPUS

Octopus briareus

Octopuses have eight arms and are adapted to living on the seabed. *Octopus briareus* is one of several species that occur on reefs in the area but is seen only at night, when it comes out to hunt. It is often pale bluish-green in colour, but can change hue within seconds. It has a hawk-like beak, which it uses to crush molluscs and other shelled animals, and often spreads its body over its prey in a parachute-like fashion. Like other cephalopods the female lays clusters of hundreds of eggs in recesses on the reef, which she guards until they hatch; she then dies. The male dies shortly after mating. This species is common on reefs throughout the region and has a maximum arm spread of about 60cm (2ft).

CRUSTACEANS

Crustaceans are incredibly numerous on coral reefs although many, being small, are overlooked. They can be found in all habitats, floating in open water (zooplankton), digging in sand, hiding among corals or crawling out in the open. Typically, they have segmented bodies with a calcareous outer skeleton. The legs are jointed and many of the crustaceans that divers see belong to the order *Decapoda* – meaning ten legs. These appendages are modified and used for a variety of purposes, including walking, swimming, defence, food capture, respiration and carrying eggs.

1 PARASITIC ISOPOD

Anilocra sp.

This parasitic crustacean belongs to the order *Isopoda*. It has a fairly flat, oval-shaped, multi-jointed body with small legs. *Anilocra* species are external parasites on a wide range of fish species, clinging on with sharp claws and damaging the tissue below, but they do not cause the death of their host. They change sex from male to female, and it is the larger females that are nearly always seen. A number of *Anilocra* species occur in the region but they are difficult to identify without the aid of a microscope.

1 Rough Fileclam

1 Caribbean Reef Squid

2 Caribbean Reef Octopus

1 Parasitic Isopod

2 SWOLLEN-CLAW MANTIS
Gonodactylus oerstedii
Mantis shrimps belong to the order Stomatopoda. They are unique among crustaceans in that the front part of the head (bearing the eyes and antennules) moves independently from the rest. The second pair of legs is adapted to seize prey. They are normally folded up, but can be extended and then snapped shut into a special groove. A mantis shrimp strike is as fast as lightening and carried out with such ferocity that it can cut other shrimps clean in half. *G. oerstedii* is one of several species of mantis shrimp that occur on reefs in the region. It reaches a length of about 5cm (2in) and its front claws lack spines but have a distinctly swollen base. It is seen occasionally on shallow to moderately deep reefs throughout the region but is shy and retreats into recesses if disturbed.

3 BANDED CORAL SHRIMP
Stenopus hispidus
This shrimp occurs on reefs throughout the Indo-Pacific as well as the western Atlantic. It has prominent red and white striped claws (chelae), and long white antennae, which are waved like flags to attract clients. Cleaning stations are close to the crevices, ledges and caves in which the shrimps live. Adult males and females live in pairs that may be stable for several years, and on reaching maturity they produce batches of eggs at regular intervals. Much of the cleaning is done at night. This species reaches a length of about 5cm (2in).

4 PEPPERMINT SHRIMP
Lysmata wurdemanni
Two species of *Lysmata* occur in the region, both can be seen occasionally on reefs from shallow water to depths of about 27cm (89ft). *L. grabhami* is reddish with a distinctive white line running along the its back, while *L. wurdemanni* has a pinkish body with red longitudinal lines. It generally lives within tubular sponges, particularly those of the genus *Aplysina*, and perches just inside the tube, waving its long antennae back and forth to attract fish. It is quite a shy species and retreats if disturbed. Its maximum length is about 4.5cm (1¾in).

5 SQUAT ANEMONE SHRIMP
Thor amboinensis
This distinctive species is brown with white saddles and spots, white eyes, short antennae and an upturned tail. It lives in association with anemones, especially the giant anemone (*Condylactis gigantea*) and sun anemone (*Stichodactyla helianthus*). If disturbed or threatened it dives into the tentacles for protection. Its maximum length is about 1cm (½in)

6 PEDERSON CLEANER SHRIMP
Periclimenes pedersoni
P. pedersoni is up to 2.5cm (1in) long, and has a transparent body with purplish-blue spots. The legs are also purplish-blue and are circled with white bands. It lives in association with a number of species of anemone, particularly the corkscrew anemone *Bartholomea annulata*. Like other *Periclimenes* species it has long, white, very thin antennae, which it waves to attract passing fish. With patience it can be enticed on to bare hands in its search for morsels of dead skin. This species is common throughout the region, from shallow water to depths of about 20m (66ft).

7 WIRE CORAL SHRIMP
Pseudopontonoides princips
Many crustaceans living on coral reefs live in association with other organisms. The wire coral shrimp is found on the branches of black corals such as *Cirrhipathes gracilis* and *Antipathes pennacea*. This cryptically coloured species is well camouflaged and can be easily overlooked. It occurs in the western Caribbean and northern Gulf of Mexico from about 15–75m (50–250ft), depending on the distribution of its hosts.

8 SPOTTED CLEANER SHRIMP
Periclimenes yucatanicus
This shrimp has several white and brown patches on its transparent body, and white spots along the side. The long, fine antennae are white with brown bands. It grows to about 2.5cm (1in) in length and can be found among the tentacles of anemones such as the giant and corkscrew anemones. Like other commensal crustaceans it is not stung by its host.

2 Swollen-claw Mantis

3 Banded Coral Shrimp

4 Peppermnt Shrimp

4 Squat Anemone Shrimp

5 Penderson Cleaner Shrimp

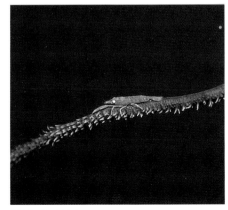

7 Wire Coral Shrimp

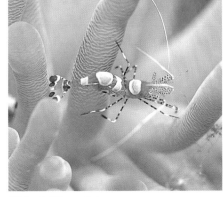

8 Spotted Cleaner Shrimp

9 RED SNAPPING SHRIMP
Alpheus armatus
Shrimps belonging to the genus *Alpheus* have fairly stout bodies with asymmetrical first legs. Each of these bears a pincer, but one is greatly enlarged and the end joint can be locked open and then suddenly released to snap shut with great force, producing the familiar pistol-shot noise. This serves two functions. It acts as a message to other shrimps not to trespass on occupied territory, and also is capable of stunning small fish. These are then pounced on and dragged back into the shrimp's lair. Generally, all that is visible of the 5cm (2in) long *Alpheus armatus* are its long red-and-white banded antennae. The rest of the body is hidden close to the column of the corkscrew anemone, or in a small chamber it excavates nearby. It is common throughout the region, occurring mainly on shallow reefs.

10 RED NIGHT SHRIMP
Rhynchocinetes rigens
As its name implies, this is a nocturnal species. By day it hides deep within the framework of the reef, but at night it is often one of the most frequently encountered animals. It reaches a length of about 5cm (2in) and can be recognized by its large, black eyes, which glow red if lit up by a torch. The body is mainly red, with a scattering of pale dots and bands. The red night shrimp occurs on shallow to medium-depth reefs throughout the region.

11 CARIBBEAN SPINY LOBSTER
Panulirus argus
Spiny lobsters (crawfish) are commonly found at the back of caves on the deeper reef, where holes and recesses provide shelter. They emerge at night to scavenge and feed on invertebrates. The carapace and antennae of *P. argus* are covered with sharp spines and the overall colour is brownish with a scattering of dark spots on the carapace and pale spots on the abdomen. The rock lobster *P. guttatus* is smaller and has a darker body with numerous white spots. Spiny lobsters have long antennae that can be moved rapidly up and down to produce a squeaking sound that keeps other lobsters out of their territory. Spiny lobsters grow to a length of 60cm (2ft). The female carries bundles of orange eggs under the abdomen and should never be collected.

12 SCULPTURED SLIPPER LOBSTER
Parribacus antarcticus
Slipper lobsters hide in crevices by day and emerge at night to forage out in the open. The flattened, plate-like appendages at the front end of the animal are modified antennae. A small, second pair of antennae protrudes from between them. These animals have no claws and feed mostly on soft-bodied animals. Several species occur in the region. *P. antarcticus* can usually be identified by the rough texture of the antennae and carapace. It occurs in warm waters throughout both the western Atlantic and Indo-Pacific.

13 GIANT HERMIT CRAB
Petrochirus diogenes
This is the largest of the Caribbean hermit crabs, with a body up to 30cm (12in) long. It often inhabits queen conch shells, and is generally found on seagrass beds in the vicinity of reefs. It is a scavenger on recently dead animals and also feeds on shelled invertebrates. The eyes of this species are blue or greenish and the antennae are red-and-white banded. Its claws are large and reddish in colour, with the right one slightly bigger than the left. It is seen occasionally throughout the region, from shallow water to depths of about 30m (98ft).

14 RED REEF HERMIT CRAB
Paguristes cadenati
Of the many species of hermit crab in the region, *P. cadenati* can usually be recognized by its yellow eyestalks, bluish-black eyes and bright red legs and carapace, adorned with occasional white spots. It grows to about 2.5cm (1in) and lives in discarded gastropod shells that are normally encrusted with red crustose algae. It may gather in small aggregations during the day, but like other hermit crabs it is seen more often at night, when it is out scavenging for food and may be seen climbing up fire corals and hydroids. This species is common throughout the region, mainly at depths between about 7m (23ft) and 30m (98ft).

9 Red Snapping Shrimp

10 Red Night Shrimp

11 Caribbean Spiny Lobster

12 Sculptured Slipper Lobster

13 Giant Hermit Crab

14 Red Reef Hermit Crab

15 CHANNEL CLINGING CRAB
Mithrax spinosissimus
Several species of *Mithrax* occur in the region. All have long legs and pincers, and are sometimes referred to as spider crabs. *M. spinosissimus* is much the largest, with a carapace width up to about 18cm (7in). It has a brownish body and legs, with paler pincers, and the carapace is often covered with algae and encrusting organisms. This species is more likely to be seen at night when it emerges from caves and other hiding places to scavenge on the reef. It is found throughout the region, from depths of 3m (10ft) to 10m (130ft).

16 YELLOWLINE ARROW CRAB
Stenorhynchus seticornis
This unmistakable crab has very long, spidery legs with a spread of over 6cm (2⅓in). Its body is held above the seabed and is small and triangular with a long, tapering rostrum. Sometimes, tufts of algae grow at the tip of the rostrum. The body is golden brown and the small pinchers usually have blue or violet tips. Burrowing worms form a major part of the diet of the arrow crab, which will even tackle the poisonous fireworm *Hermodice* and consume it without any apparent problem. Some of the arrow worms seen on the reef have one or more limbs missing, but

these can be re-grown quite quickly – a useful survival mechanism in the tough environment of the reef. This species is common throughout the region, occurring in many habitats, from shallow water to depths of 40m (130ft).

17 CRYPTIC TEARDROP CRAB
Pelia mutica
This crab is one of a number of crabs that have the habit of disguising themselves with other organisms so that they resemble a piece of the reef rather than a potential meal for predators. They do this by picking up small pieces of sponge, algae or other items in their claws and then placing them on the body. The fragments are held in place with tiny hooked hairs (setae) which, once attached, continue to grow normally. However, if the crab moves to a different background it will replace any non-matching pieces with more suitable ones so that it maintains its disguise. These crabs are so confident of not being recognized that they remain motionless if approached, rather than trying to scuttle into a crevice. The carapace and legs of *Pelia mutica* are heavily decorated with sponges but the bluish-purple pincers are usually visible. This species is common throughout the region, occurring in most reef habitats. The carapace width is about 2cm (⅚in).

BRYOZOANS

Bryozoans occur widely on reefs, but are inconspicuous and often overlooked. The range of form and size of the colonies is often greater in shady places such as caves, steep walls and the undersides of corals. Some are rigid, encrusting types (calcareous or soft), others form delicate fan-like structures that are extremely beautiful although delicate and easily broken. There may also be hanging tufts, resembling filamentous red algae at first glance. On close examination it is possible to see a mosaic of tiny, 1mm (0.04in) diameter, cubicles over the surface, which mark the position of each individual animal (zooid) that makes up the colony. These animals are filter feeders, drawing water into the body using ciliated tentacles at the head end.

1 WHITE FAN BRYOZOAN
Reteporellina evelinae
Unlike most of the other species of lacy bryozoan likely to be seen in the area, the white fan bryozoan is calcareous and fairly inflexible. It has a beautiful structure consisting of

highly-divided narrow fronds. Colonies are seldom larger than 5cm (2in) in diameter. They can be found from depths of about 7–30m (25–100ft) in sheltered, shady situations, such as cave walls and recesses in the reef.

15 Channel Clinging Crab

16 Yellowline Arrow Crab

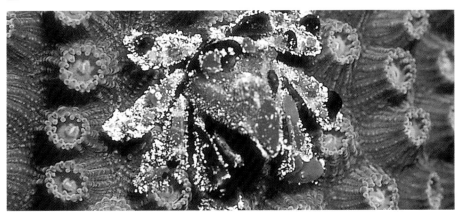

17 Cryptic Teardrop Crab

1 White Fan Bryozoan

ECHINODERMS

Echinoderms are a very important group of animals that occur only in the marine environment. There are many different forms, but all have an internal skeleton of small calcareous plates, and a water vascular system consisting of fluid-filled canals. Tiny tube feet are a part of this system and are used for locomotion and capturing food.

BRITTLE STARS AND BASKET STARS

1 SPONGE BRITTLE STAR
Ophiothrix suensonii
Like all brittle stars, the sponge brittle star has long, slender arms with a small central body. The arms may be deliberately shed if the animal is disturbed or attacked, and replacements can be grown. The tube feet that line the arms are used for capturing planktonic food. This species lives in association with sponges, fire coral and sometimes gorgonians. Its arms are up to 12cm (4¾in) length and the disk 2cm (¾in) in diameter. It is common on reefs throughout the area, from surface waters to depths of several hundred metres.

2 GIANT BASKET STAR
Astrophyton muricatum
The basket star is a specialized type of brittlestar with thin, branched arms that are adapted for filter feeding. During the day, basket stars are curled into a tight ball and hidden from view beneath corals and in crevices. At night they emerge, unfurl the arms and start feeding (torchlight causes them to recoil). on plankton such as crustacean larvae, which are then restrained using tiny hooks. The basket star is common on reefs throughout the region.

STARFISH

1 CUSHION SEA STAR
Oreaster reticulatus
The cushion star is easily recognized by its heavy build and short, pointed arms. There are usually five arms, but may be only four, or as many as seven. It is brownish in colour with numerous blunt spines (tubercles) arranged in a network on its upper surface. This is the largest starfish in the region, growing to 50cm (1ft 8in) in diameter. It feeds mainly on bivalve molluscs, and is common on seagrass beds and shallow, sandy habitats throughout the region.

SEA URCHINS

Sea urchins have a body enclosed in a test or shell consisting of closely fitting calcium carbonate plates. This is armed with numerous spines, which in many species are toxic. The spines are attached to the test by a type of ball-and-socket joint and are highly mobile. Along with the tube feet, they help the urchin to move, as well as defend it from predators.

1 VARIEGATED URCHIN
Lytechinus variegatus
This species is found mainly on reefs and in seagrass beds or sandy habitats. It has a habit known as 'hatting' in which it places pieces of seagrass or broken mollusc shell on its upper surface, presumably either as camouflage or to protect it from bright light. This species is usually whitish in colour, occasionally shades of green or purple, and has white tube feet. The spines are fairly short, and the urchin grows to about 7.5cm (3in) in diameter. It occurs throughout the region from shallow reefs to depths of about 15m (49ft). Like other urchins it feeds by grazing algae off the reef surface.

2 WEST INDIAN SEA EGG
Tripneustes ventricosus
T. ventricosus is the largest sea urchin in the area, occasionally reaching a diameter of 15cm (6in). Its test is dark, and covered in short, white spines. Between the spines are minute, poisonous pincers called pedicellaria, which the animal uses for defence. The sea egg is active only at night, grazing on algae, seagrasses and the thin layers of organic detritus coating the top of the sand. However, it may be spotted during the day, partially concealed beneath a shady 'hat' of seagrass and algal fragments and pieces of shell. The sea egg occurs on seagrass beds and shallow rocky areas throughout the region. The gonads of this species are considered a delicacy, and this has led to over-harvesting in some places.

1 Sponge Brittle Star

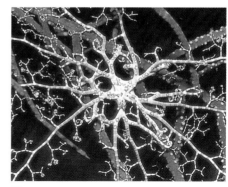

2 Giant Basket Star

1 Cushion Sea Star

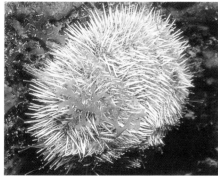

1 Variegated Urchin

2 West Indian Sea Egg

3 LONG-SPINED URCHIN
Diadema antillarum

This species is in the family *Diadematidae*, a group of urchins with long, poisonous, needle-like spines. The test in *D. antillarum* is up to about 7.5cm (3in) in diameter, and the spines may reach 20cm (8in). Adults are black throughout, but the juvenile may have white-banded spines. The outside of the spines is coated with poisonous mucus, which causes considerable discomfort if the spines penetrate the skin and become embedded in the flesh. Long-spined urchins are common and some-times abundant throughout the region, occur-ring from shallow water to depths of 40m (130ft). They usually aggregate in shady crevices and holes during the day, emerging at night to graze on algae. They play an important ecological role in keeping algal growth in check.

4 MAGNIFICENT URCHIN
Astropyga magnifica

This distinctive species is another member of the family *Diadematidae*, but has shorter spines than *D. antillarum*. Juveniles have a pinkish body with reddish-banded spines. The adults are a uniform darkish purple in colour. The spines in this species are arranged in five sectors with gaps between them. This is a fair-ly rare, deep-water urchin, occurring on reefs at depths below about 20m (66ft). The test grows to about 13cm (5in) in diameter and the spines are up to 11cm (4¼in) long.

5 REEF URCHIN
Echinometra viridis

The body of this urchin is dark reddish in colour, and the spines are paler but with dark tips. The test may reach about 5cm (2in) in diameter, and the spines are always slightly shorter than the test diameter but are relatively longer than those of the closely related boring urchin *Echinometra lucunter*. *E. viridis* hides beneath rocks and corals during the day, while *E. lucunter* sits snugly inside a hole that it makes for itself in the rock. Both species emerge at night to graze on algae. The reef urchin is absent from the eastern Caribbean islands, but is fairly common on shal-low reefs elsewhere.

6 SLATE-PENCIL URCHIN
Eucidaris tribuloides

This species is easily recognised by its thick, blunt spines which are usually coated in a thin layer of filamentous algae or small encrusting organisms. The spines are widely spaced and about the same length as the diameter of the test, which reaches a maximum of 5cm (2in). The slate-pencil urchin occurs throughout the area, from shallow water to depths of about 23m (75ft) and is especially common on sea-grass beds. It can also be found in rubble and reef areas, but often is hidden out of view in a crevice. Like other sea urchins, this species is a grazer. It feeds on algae, seagrass and sponges, moving slowly using the spines around the mouth for locomotion.

HOLOTHURIANS

1 TIGER TAIL SEA CUCUMBER
Holothuria thomasi

Sea cucumbers are bilaterally symmetrical echinoderms with a front and a rear end. Typ-ically, they are in the shape of a cucumber, and most roam over the seabed or burrow in sand. They feed either on sediment or plankton. Sev-eral species of *Holothuria* occur in the region. The body of *H. thomasi* is up to 2m (6ft 7in) long, and resembles the hose of a vacuum cleaner. It hides during the day and partially emerges at night. The posterior end remains attached under rocks; the anterior end has tentacles with leaf or disk-shaped (peltate) ends, which are in almost constant use mop-ping up particles of organic detritus from the sand (or rock) surface. This species occurs on reefs throughout the region, from shallow water to depths of about 30m (98ft).

3 Long-spined Urchin

4 Magnificent Urchin

5 Reef Urchin

6 Slate Pencil Urchin

6 Tiger Tail Sea Cucumber

ASCIDIANS

Ascidians (sea squirts or tunicates) do not look like particularly advanced animals, yet they are closely related to vertebrates. The tail of the tiny planktonic larva is strengthened with a rod-like structure very similar to the vertebrate backbone, and the gullet (pharynx) of the adult is perforated like the gills of fish.

1 PAINTED TUNICATE

Clavelina picta

This species is an example of a solitary ascidian, although it usually grows in clusters of several or hundreds of individuals joined at the base by stolons. The base is attached to the rocks or to animals such as gorgonians and sponges. At the top end are two openings. Water is drawn in through the incurrent siphon and over the gill net in the pharynx, where planktonic food and oxygen are removed. It then flows out through the exhalent siphon. The body of this species is usually transparent or translucent with the incurrent siphon ringed in white or purple. It is found throughout the region from shallow water to depths of over 30m (98ft).

2 WHITE SPECK TUNICATE

Didemnum conchyliatum

Didemnum conchyliatum is one of the many colonial species that occurs in the region. Numerous tiny, individual zooids are embedded in a common tunic that is yellowish in colour and up to about 5cm (2in) in diameter. The inhalant openings are visible as tiny holes, while the exhalent apertures open into a common, larger opening known as the cloaca. These openings contract and close if the animal is disturbed. *D. conchyliatum* can be distinguished by the tiny white spicules that are embedded in its tissue giving it a speckled appearance. It occurs throughout the region on shallow to deep reefs, attached either to rocks or reef organisms such as the elephant ear sponge.

3 GIANT TUNICATE

Polycarpa spongiabilis

P. spongiabilis is a solitary species consisting of a single zooid. It is sac-shaped, with two openings. These siphons are very obvious, and protrude slightly above the general body surface. The one on the top is the ingoing (inhalent) siphon and the one on the side carries the outgoing stream of water. The fringe of tentacles just inside the inhalent siphon are not branched in this species, which distinguish it from similar species which have branched tentacles. As the name implies, this is a large species, reaching a height of about 10cm (4in). The outside is often camouflaged by pieces of algae or debris. It occurs on reefs throughout the area, from shallow water to depths of about 30m (98ft). The common name 'seasquirt' is derived from the behavior of this group of animals if they are taken from the water or stranded at low tide. The body of the animal contracts, resulting in a stream of water being pushed out through the siphons.

4 BLUEBELL TUNICATE

Clavelina puertosecensis

Like other Clavelina species, the blue bell tunicate consists of a clump of individuals joined at the base. The zooids are smaller than in other members of the genus, reaching a maximum height of only about 1.25cm (½in). Colour ranges from blue to transluscent or greenish, and generally the rim of the zooid is pale. This species is seen occasionally on reefs throughout the area, from shallow water to depths of about 30m (98ft).

1 Painted Tunicate

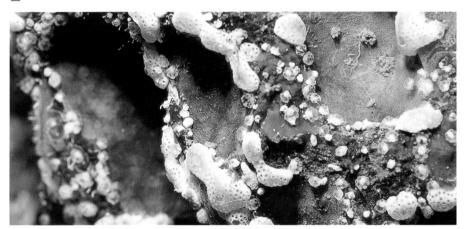

2 White Speck Tunicate

3 Giant Tunicate

4 Bluebell Tunicate

FISH

SHARKS

Sharks are sometimes referred to as primitive fish because of features such as their cartilaginous skeleton. Yet they are highly successful animals whose forbears were thriving in our oceans up to 100 million years ago. All sharks eat living animals, but their food varies from zooplankton to molluscs, fish and turtles. Several species are more active at night than during the day. In addition to a reflective device in their eyes that increases sensitivity in dim light, they are also able to detect low-level electric fields, and so can home in on sleeping fish. Their lateral line system is also well developed, consisting of a row of tiny holes that connect with the fluid-filled canals that house the sense cells. With this pressure-sensitive system they are able to detect low frequency vibrations occurring a considerable distance away. The sense of 'smell' in sharks is sophisticated.

1 WHALE SHARK
Rhincodon typus

The whale shark is the largest fish in the world, generally reaching a length of about 12m (39ft), but sometimes several metres longer. It is easily recognized by the spots on the dorsal surface, white belly and wide, toothless mouth. Large individuals tend to be solitary, but the smaller ones may move around in groups. *Ecology*: occurs in all tropical areas, and may occasionally be seen around Caribbean reefs. This shark may migrate considerable distances in search of food, moving towards plankton blooms wherever they develop.

2 NURSE SHARK
Ginglymostoma cirratum

The nurse shark has a small mouth with a barbel extending from below each nostril. It has two fairly close-set dorsal fins that are nearly equal in size, and situated towards the rear of the body. Maximum length is about 4m (13ft). *Ecology*: occurs on and around reefs throughout the region, from shallow water to depths of 35m (115ft), and spends much of its time resting in caves or beneath ledges. It feeds on molluscs and crustaceans and will not attack divers unless provoked.

3 REEF SHARK
Carcharhinus perezii

All species of the genus *Carcharhinus* have sleek bodies and two dorsal fins of unequal size. The first is larger and situated above the ventral fin while the second is much smaller. The upper lobe of the tail fin is much larger than the lower one. *C. perezii* reaches a length of about 3m (9ft 10in) and has a dusky margin to the ventral, anal and tail fins that distinguishes it from a similar species, the bull shark *C. leucas*. *Ecology*: occurs on and around reefs throughout the region, from shallow water to depths of about 65m (215ft). It may cruise singly or in groups, and is sometimes seen resting on the bottom. Although generally shy, it is considered to be a dangerous species.

4 BLACKTIP SHARK
Carcharhinus limbatus

This species has black tips to the fins, but these sometimes fade with age. There is a white stripe along the side of its silvery body. It grows to a length of 2.5m (8ft 3in). *Ecology*: occurs in warm waters around the globe. Juveniles may be seen off beaches while adults are primarily open water hunters, but sometimes visits reefs when following prey such as mackerel. It is considered potentially dangerous.

1 Whale Shark

2 Nurse Shark

3 Reef Shark

4 Blacktip Shark

SILKY SHARK
Carcharhinus falciformis

This species gets its name from the skin, which is relatively smooth. It has a slender, grey body without any distinctive markings, and may reach 2.5m (8ft 3in) in length. Like other sharks, males and females show courtship behaviour and practice internal fertilisation.

Female silky sharks, along with a number of other species, develop a placenta for the nutrition of the developing litter. Up to fourteen young may be developing in the female at any one time. *Ecology*: occurs in warm waters around the globe. It is oceanic but may occasionally visit outer reefs while hunting. Juveniles in particular tend to move in schools and often associate with tuna.

RAYS

These fish have a distinctive outline in which the pectoral fin is continuous with the head. They are flattened from top to bottom and the mouth is on the underside. Like sharks, rays also have a cartilaginous skeleton.

1 LESSER ELECTRIC RAY
Narcine brasiliensis

The head and body of the electric ray are rounded and the tail is short. This species grows to a length of about 45cm (1ft 6in) and is greyish brown with darker blotches. There is an electric organ on each side of the disk, which produces a mild electric shock (usually less than 35 volts). *Ecology*: occurs along mainland coasts but is rarely seen north of Tobago. It is usually buried in sand with only its eyes protruding, so can be easily overlooked. Like other electric rays, this species eats fish, which it envelops and then stuns with its electric organ.

2 SOUTHERN STINGRAY
Dasyatis americana

The southern stingray has an angular disk up to about 1.5m (5ft) across the 'wings'. It is brownish or grey in colour, with a white underside. The tail is long and, like all stingrays, it has one or two long spines near its base. *Ecology*: occurs in shallow sandy areas adjacent to reefs and is found throughout the region. It usually lies on the bottom covered in sand, with just the eyes and spiracles (gill openings) visible.

Feeding is mostly at dusk and dawn and often pits can be seen in the sand where molluscs have been hunted out.

The venomous tail spines are used for defence but are seldom a hazard for divers. Rays in places such as 'Sting Ray City' in the Cayman Islands engage in many close encounters with humans, yet their antics seldom lead to injury. The main danger is for people wading with bare feet in shallow areas. A stingray's reaction when trodden on is to lash its tail up and forward, neatly impaling the foot before it can be lifted away.

3 YELLOW STINGRAY
Urolophus jamaicensis

This species has an almost round disk up to 76cm (2ft 6in) across, and a fairly short tail with a spine at the end. It is yellowish brown with numerous pale and dark spots. *Ecology*: seen occasionally in most parts of the region where it occurs in shallow sandy areas adjacent to reefs. It may be partially or completely buried and will remain still if divers do not approach too closely. When feeding it often arches the front of the body up to form what appears to other fish as a suitable shelter to hide in. Once in this treacherous tunnel, their fate is sealed.

4 Silky Shark

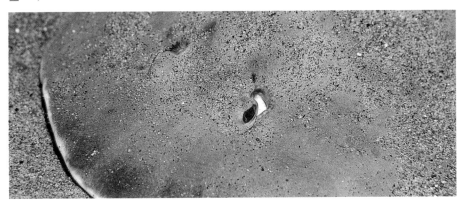

1 Lesser Electric Ray

2 Southern Stingray

3 Yellow Stingray

4 SPOTTED EAGLE RAY
Aetobatus narinari

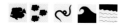

The eagle ray has long, triangular 'wings' up to about 2.4m (8ft) across and a long tail. Its head is pointed, which immediately distinguishes it from the manta ray. The dorsal surface is dark, with white spots. *Ecology:* occurs in tropical waters around the globe. It feeds on large, attached shells such as oysters and clams, and may also dig for sand-dwelling crustaceans and molluscs, using its plate-like teeth to crush the shells. Unlike other rays it spends much of its time cruising in open water around the reef and only descends periodically to the bottom in search of prey.

5 MANTA RAY
Manta birostris

Manta birostris has a maximum 'wingspan' of around 6.7m (22ft). It has two large horn-like flaps on its head and a wide mouth situated right at the front of the head. Its dorsal surface is darkish with pale markings. Another manta species, the devil ray *Mobula hypostoma* is smaller, has a dark back without markings and a mouth that is set back from the front of the head. *Ecology:* occurs in warm waters around the globe and is an occasional visitor to plankton-rich areas of the reef. It uses the distinctive cephalic flaps on the front of the head to direct a stream of plankton-laden water into the mouth. When the mood takes them, they can leap clean out of the water.

EELS

MORAY EELS

Moray eels are elongate fish with continuous dorsal and anal fins that join up with the tail fin. They have no pectoral fins. Many species of moray eel occur on the reef, although they are often hidden in holes during the day, with only the head showing. They have sharply pointed canine teeth, suited to their fish eating habits, and hunting is done mostly at night. They locate their prey mainly through smell, by drawing water into sensitive nostrils located on the front of the head. The constant opening and closing of the mouth seen in many species is not a sign of imminent attack, but merely an action that pumps water over the gills for respiration.

1 GREEN MORAY
Gymnothorax funebris

This is the largest moray in the region, reaching a length of 1.8m (6ft). It is a uniform olive green in colour. *Ecology:* occurs on reefs and a range of other habitats such as mangroves and seagrass beds. It is common throughout the region from shallow water to depths of over 40m (30ft).

2 SPOTTED MORAY
Gymnothorax moringa

This species has a pale body densely covered with small, dark spots. It reaches a length of about 1.2m (4ft). *Ecology:* occurs on coral and rocky reefs throughout the region, from shallow to deep water.

3 GOLDENTAIL MORAY
Gymnothorax miliaris

The yellow tail of this species is diagnostic, although unfortunately it is often concealed. The rest of the body is brownish with numerous small, dark dots. It grows to about 60cm (2ft) in length. *Ecology:* occurs on and around reefs throughout the area, to depths of about 60m (195ft).

4 Spotted Eagle Ray

5 Manta Ray

1 Green Moray

2 Spotted Moray

3 Goldentail Moray

CHAIN MORAY

Echidna catenata

E. catenata is easily distinguished by its dark body with bright yellow markings. It reaches a maximum length of about 70cm (2ft 4in). *Ecology*: a shallow water species, occurring throughout the region on reefs to a depth of about 12m (39ft).

VIPER MORAY
Enchelychore nigricans

This species has jaws that arch away from each other and prominent teeth. It is brownish in colour and usually slightly mottled. *Ecology*: occurs throughout the region on coral and rocky reefs to a depth of about 30m (98ft).

SNAKE EELS – OPHICHTHIDAE

1 SHARPTAIL EEL
Myrichthys breviceps

The sharptail eel has a greyish body with pale blotches, and smaller yellow spots on the head. The fins are small and inconspicuous, making the fish look very snake-like. *M. breviceps* grows to a length of about 90cm (3ft)

Several species of snake eel occur in the area. *Ecology:* The sharptail eel occurs in shallow sandy habitats throughout the region, but is seldom seen because of its secretive habits. It hides in dark holes or in sand during the day, sometimes with its head visible. At night it becomes more active, possibly to coincide with the emergence of small prey organisms from the sand around its burrow. A few species actually leave their burrows and holes to forage elsewhere.

GARDEN EELS – HETEROCONGRIDAE

1 BROWN GARDEN EEL
Heteroconger halis

The garden eel has a thin, brownish or grey body, which is up to 50cm (1ft 8in) long. *Ecology*: this species occurs throughout the region, from depths of 5 to 40m (16 to 130ft). It lives in large colonies at current-swept sites, often on sand plains at mid-depth (for example on sandy terraces, or on deeper slopes). The body, seldom thicker than a finger, projects from the sand and moves in a graceful, wave-like movement as the fish searches out and snaps up plankton. Garden eels are very sensitive to the presence of divers and retreat rapidly into their burrows when frightened.

TARPON
FAMILY MEGALOPIDAE

1 TARPON
Megalops atlanticus

The tarpon is a silvery fish that grows to a length of 2.4m (8ft). It has a distinctive, upturned mouth and a single dorsal fin with a long filament extending from the rear end.

Ecology: occurs throughout the region in a wide range of shallow water habitats including bays, estuaries and coral reefs. During the day it often forms large schools, and these tend to occupy specific reef localities for years at a time. Tarpon are relatively unconcerned by divers. They may hunt during the day, but are more active at night.

4 Chain Moray

5 Viper Moray

1 Sharptail Eel

1 Brown Garden Eel

1 Tarpon

SILVERSIDES
FAMILY ANTENNARIIDAE

Members of this family are small fish with a narrow body, a silvery mid-lateral band down the body, a forked tail, two dorsal fins and a small terminal mouth. *Ecology*: several similar-looking species of silverside occur in the region, and there are also species of herring, anchovy and sardine that look very similar and cannot be identified underwater. Silversides usually form large schools and can be seen drifting in sheltered areas of the reef such as canyons and caves. They feed on zooplankton.

LIZARDFISH
FAMILY SYNODONTIDAE

1 SAND DIVER
Synodus intermedius

Lizardfish, also sometimes known as 'grinners', have a large, wide mouth full of sharp teeth, even on the tongue. They have cylindrical, slender bodies and two dorsal fins – one is large and prominent, the other tiny. Of the four species that occur in the area, *S. intermedius* is the commonest, and can usually be recognized by the dark spot on the top edge of the gill cover, the reddish-brown bars and thin yellow stripes along the body. *Ecology*: the sand diver is common in sandy areas and on reefs throughout the region from shallow water to depths of over 40m (130ft). It may bury itself in sand, or perch on rocks and coral, lying in wait for small fish and shrimps, which they pounce on with incredible speed.

CLINGFISH
FAMILY GOBIESOCIDAE

1 RED CLINGFISH
Arcos rubiginosus

The red clingfish is a small, highly specialized fish with a ventral sucking disk formed from its greatly modified pelvic fins. The body is flattened, scaleless and covered with a thick coat of mucus. *Ecology*: there are a few species present in the Caribbean and all live in and around the reef. Venturing out at night to feed, they 'cling' to rope sponges and the underside of dead corals, darting out to pick at passing plankton or small crustaceans. Difficult to spot, they are a rare and interesting find on the reef.

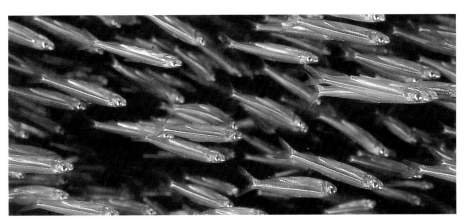

Silversides

1 Sand Diver

1 Red Clingfish

TOADFISH
FAMILY AULOSTOMIDAE

Toadfish get their name from the 'croaking' sounds they make to attract mates. They are bottom-dwelling fish that have a large head and mouth and a single long dorsal fin with three spines at the anterior end. The mouth is often fringed with flaps of tissue, and the body is stoutly built and lacks scales. Several species of toadfish occur in the region.

3 SPLENDID TOADFISH
Sanopus splendidus

This species is easily recognized by the black and white stripes on its head, yellow pectoral fins and yellow margins to the other fins. It reaches a length of about 20cm (8in). *Ecology:* most reef fish have planktonic larvae and are widely distributed, but this species is most common around the Mexican island of Cozumel. It occurs close to or inside holes and crevices on reefs at 10 to 25m (33 to 82ft).

2 LARGE EYE TOADFISH
Batrachoides gilberti

The large eye and branched barbels around the mouth help to identify this species. It reaches a maximum length of about 25cm (9¾in) and is brownish in colour. *Ecology:* occurs only along the coastline of central America, and not in the wider Caribbean. It may occasionally be seen on reefs but is more common in shallow water habitats such as mangroves and creeks.

ANGLERFISH
FAMILY ANTENNARIIDAE

Anglerfish (or frogfish) have a bulbous body with a large, upturned mouth. The pectoral fins are jointed and used for 'walking' on the seabed, and the first dorsal fin is modified to form a fishing rod with a lure at its tip. This apparatus is jiggled around to attract other fish, which are then eaten whole. Anglerfish have loose, flabby skin and a body than can distend to accommodate prey larger than themselves. Mature females lay a mass of eggs on the seabed every few days. Several species of anglerfish occur in the area but they are well camouflaged and often overlooked.

1 LONGLURE FROGFISH
Antennarius multiocellatus

This species has many dark spots on its body, and three particularly obvious ones on its tail. Larger than other species, it reaches a length of about 20cm (8in), and has a long fishing rod. *Ecology:* common on reefs throughout the region, occurring at most depths but most frequently on the reef top where it often associates with sponges, blending in with them so as to be almost invisible. This means that potential prey are unaware of the fish's presence and investigate the lure without fear – but to their cost! .

2 SARGASSUMFISH
Histrio histrio

The sargassumfish is one of the most bizarre members of the frogfish family, and the only one to have a pelagic existence. Its body is covered with leafy and fleshy appendages closely resembling the shapes of the sargassum weed in which it lives. Mottled brown and yellow colouration complete the camouflage. *Ecology:* widespread in all tropical waters except the eastern Pacific. It is seen occasionally among floating sargassum weed in surface waters of the Caribbean region.

1 Splendid Toadfish

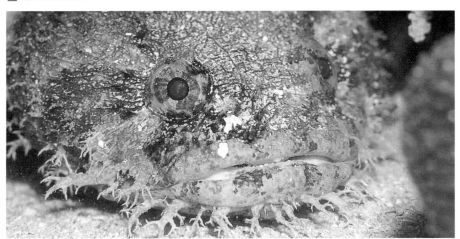

2 Large Eye Toadfish

1 Longlure Frogfish

2 Sargassumfish

SQUIRRELFISH and SOLDIERFISH
FAMILY HOLOCENTRIDAE

These are medium-sized, deep-bodied fish with large eyes and stout spines on the fins. They are mainly red in colour. Squirrelfish are distinguished from soldierfish by the presence of a large spine on the cheek. All members of this family rest during the day in or around caves, underhangs, crevices and among corals. At night they become active and disperse in search of food. Soldierfish feed mostly on zooplankton while squirrelfish forage over rubble, sand and seagrass for invertebrates and small fish, such as cardinalfish.

1 SQUIRRELFISH
Holocentrus adscensionis

This species is identified by the white or yellowish tips to the spiny dorsal fin. It reaches a length of about 30cm (12in). *Ecology*: very common on reefs throughout the region, from shallow water to depths of 50m (165ft).

2 LONGSPINE SQUIRRELFISH
Holocentrus rufus

H. rufus has an unusually long anal fin spine and white tips to the spiny dorsal. *Ecology*: common on reefs throughout the region, from shallow water to depths of at least 40m (130ft).

3 LONGJAW SQUIRRELFISH
Holocentrus marianus

This species has orange-yellow stripes on the body, a yellow bar on the gill cover and a yellow spiny dorsal fin. It is the largest of the Caribbean squirrelfish, reaching a length of 40cm (1ft 4in). *Ecology*: very common on reefs throughout the region, especially below 30m (98ft).

4 BLACKBAR SOLDIERFISH
Myripristis jacobus

Of the two species of soldierfish occurring in the area, *M. jacobus* is easily identified by the black bar just behind the gill cover. It grows to a length of about 20cm (8in). *Ecology*: seen occasionally on reefs throughout the region to depths of at least 40m (130ft).

TRUMPETFISH
FAMILY AULOSTOMIDAE

1 TRUMPETFISH
Aulostomus maculatus

The trumpetfish has an elongate body with a long, trumpet-shaped snout and small tail fin. It is sometimes confused with the cornetfish (*Fistularia tabacaria*), but the latter species has a longer, narrower snout and a very long whip-like tail. The trumpetfish reaches a length of about 100cm (3ft 3in) and exhibits a range of colour phases and patterns. *Ecology*: common on reefs throughout the area, from shallow water to depths of about 25m (82ft). Trumpetfish have a very extensible mouth and use suction to capture prey such as small fish and crustaceans. They are not agile swimmers and use stealth to make a close approach. Often, they hang upright and well concealed among the tall stems of the sea rod *Pseudoplexaura*. They have also perfected the art of shadowing larger fish such as rock cod, ready to dart at small prey, or even steal food from their 'host'.

1 Squirrelfish

2 Longspine Squirrelfish

3 Longjaw Squirrelfish

4 Blackbar Soldierfish

1 Trumpetfish

SEAHORSES and PIPEFISH
FAMILY SYNGNATHIDAE

These fish have protruding snouts and elongate bodies that are encased in bony rings. Most species are small and inconspicuous, but some of the pipefish are brightly coloured. Reproduction in seahorses and pipefish is unusual. They live in pairs and when breeding, the female deposits her eggs in her partner's brood pouch. They hatch here and the male then takes care of them until they are ready to live an independent life.

1 LONGSNOUT SEAHORSE
Hippocampus reidi

Seahorses swim upright and the head is flexed at an angle to the body so that it points forwards. The tail is curled and prehensile. *H. reidi* is variable in colour with numerous tiny black spots on its body. It reaches a maximum size of about 15cm (6in). The other species that may be encountered is the lined seahorse *H. erectus*, which lacks spots but has many narrow, dark lines on the head, neck and back. *Ecology*: occurs throughout the region, especially in sheltered habitats such as seagrass beds, lagoons and around jetties.

2 HARLEQUIN PIPEFISH
Micrognathus ensenadae

The harlequin pipefish has a long, thin body with an elongate snout and reaches a length of about 23cm (9in). A number of species of banded pipefish occur in the area, and identification can be difficult. *Ecology*: seen very occasionally on reefs throughout the area. Like other pipefish, this species is shy and secretive and can easily be overlooked. It usually keeps close to the surface of the reef, often hiding in holes and crevices or among algae or attached organisms.

SCORPIONFISH
FAMILY SCORPAENIDAE

Scorpionfish are well-built, bottom-dwelling fish that are armed with venomous dorsal, anal and pelvic fin spines. Most species camouflage themselves by mimicking the form of algae, corals and rocks. They are mottled in colour and generally have numerous flaps and tassels of tissue around the head. Scorpionfish are predators, and their aim is to make themselves inconspicuous so that they can get close to their potential prey. They have a large mouth with many sharp teeth.

1 PLUMED SCORPIONFISH
Scorpaena grandicornis

This species can be identified by the large, fleshy appendage above each eye (the only other species with long head tentacles is restricted to Brazilian waters). *S. grandicornis* is mottled brown and grows to a length of about 18cm (7in). *Ecology*: seen occasionally on shallow to mid-depth reefs from Florida to the Caribbean.

2 SPOTTED SCORPIONFISH
Scorpaena plumieri

The spotted scorpionfish is mottled, with three dark bars on the tail. It usually has numerous small flaps of skin on the head. When disturbed, this species may 'flash' or display the purple, black and white inner side of the pectoral fins. It grows to a maximum length of about 46cm (1½ft). *Ecology*: fairly common on shallow to mid-depth reefs throughout the region.

2 Harlequin Pipefish

1 Longsnout Seahorse

1 Plumed Scorpionfish

2 Spotted Scorpionfish (juvenile)

GURNARDS
FAMILY DACTYLOPTERIDAE

1 FLYING GURNARD
Dactylopterus volitans

The flying gurnard is a spectacular fish, which grows to a length of about 46 cm (18in) and is immediately recognizable by its large pectoral fins. These are normally folded against the body, but if the fish is disturbed they are spread out like wings and used for 'flying'. The pectorals are beautifully coloured, with a bluish underside and spots on the outside. The spines and rays of the pelvic fin are also modified – in this case they are not joined by membrane but are separate like toes, and used for walking across the seabed. *Ecology*: occurs in shallow, sandy and seagrass habitats throughout the region but is uncommon.

GROUPERS
FAMILY SERRANIDAE

This large family includes species that range from a few centimetres to over 2m (6ft 7in) in length. They have a single dorsal fin, with a notch between the spiny and soft part, and a characteristically jutting lower jaw and large eyes. The bigger species are robustly built and can look quite benign as they rest lazily on the seabed or drift gently close to recesses in the reef. But groupers are highly effective predators with a remarkable turn of speed when hunting. When feeding they rush at their prey, open their large mouths wide, and suck the victim into their mouth. Groupers are generally solitary and are sequential hermaphrodites. Each fish functions first as a female, then turns into a male in later life. Removal of large specimens by fishermen can thus lead to a shortage of males as well as a general decline in populations. Many groupers are fairly shy of people, but others are curious and will emerge from their den and simply stare at an approaching diver. This makes them an easy target and very vulnerable to spearfishermen.

1 JEWFISH
Epinephelus itajara

The jewfish is the largest of the western Atlantic groupers, reaching a length of about 250cm (8ft 3in). Its colour varies from pale olive to darker brown but this species is usually distinguished by the small dark spots over its body and fins, oblique bars (especially in younger fish) and rounded tail. Females mature at four to six years, around 1m (3ft 3in) long, and develop into males at six to seven years, at a length of about 135cm (4ft 5in). They are known to live for nearly 40 years, but in many places are not given the chance. Stocks have declined, especially in Florida, where spearfishing has taken a heavy toll. *Ecology*: occurs on rocky and coral reefs throughout the area, but is uncommon. It usually hides in caves and under ledges down to depths of 100m (320ft), but may also be found in seagrass and mangrove areas. Juveniles are found primarily in estuaries. Territorial jewfish and adults may take threatening postures by quivering the body and opening the mouth, and divers are occasionally stalked by large specimens. The mouth has a huge gape, and there is a legend that it was a jewfish, rather than a whale, that swallowed Jonah. However, judging from examination of their stomach contents, spiny lobsters appear to be the most favoured prey. They may also take crabs, spiny fish such as stingrays and porcupinefish, and the occasional turtle.

1 Flying Gurnard

1 Jewfish

2 NASSAU GROUPER
Epinephelus striatus

The Nassau grouper grows to 1.2m (4ft). Its colour varies from pale to almost black, depending on its environment and 'mood', but it can always be distinguished by the large black spot on top of the tail base and five irregular dark bars. *Ecology*: occurs from 1 to 35m (3 to 115ft) and may be common on shallow reefs and seagrass beds, where it often rests on the bottom, blending in with the background. This species spawns around new moon, aggregating in huge numbers (up to 30,000) at specific spawning sites. They are often subjected to heavy fishing as they migrate and spawn.

3 RED GROUPER
Epinephelus morio

E. morio can be recognized by its overall brownish-red colour with pale blotches and indistinct darker bars. It also has a higher spiny dorsal fin than other species. It grows to a maximum length of about 90cm (3ft). *Ecology*: occurs mainly on rocky reefs, from shallow water to depths of over 120m (395ft). It is most common in Florida and the Bahamas, and rarely seen in the Caribbean.

4 RED HIND
Epinephelus guttatus

This species is identified by the dark margins of the tail, soft dorsal and anal fin, together with the reddish-brown spots. It grows to a length of about 67cm (2ft 2in) and research carried out on this important fishery species shows that it matures early with around half of all specimens having passed through the female phase and become functional males by the age of three years. *Ecology*: occurs on rocky and coral reefs throughout the region, from shallow water to depths of about 80m (260ft). This species may rest motionless on the sea bottom or drift gently just above it, and can be approached quite closely.

5 GRAYSBY
Epinephelus cruentatus

The graysby is distinguished from other red-spotted species (for example, *E. guttatus* and *E. adscensionis*) by the presence of three to five dark spots along the top of the body, just below the dorsal fin. It grows to a length of about 35cm (1ft 2in). *Ecology*: this is one of the commonest of the coral hinds, occurring widely on reefs with caves and hiding places, down to depths of over 70m (230ft). It is unafraid of divers.

6 YELLOWFIN GROUPER
Mycteroperca venenosa

Body colour in this species is very variable, from reddish-brown to almost black, and colour may change quite rapidly. Rounded blotches are usually visible. The outer part of the pectoral fin is bright yellow, a feature shared by the black grouper *M. bonaci*. However, the latter has a narrower yellow margin, and rectangular-shaped rather than rounded blotches on the body. Maximum size is about 90cm (3ft). *Ecology*: occurs throughout the region on reefs from shallow water to depths of about 30m (98ft). It is often seen resting on the floor of caves and similar sheltered habitats.

7 TIGER GROUPER
Mycteroperca tigris

Like other members of this family, the tiger grouper can switch colour dramatically and may change from bright red to almost black. Normally about nine dark brown diagonal bars are clearly visible. It reaches a maximum length of about 100cm (3ft 3in). *Ecology*: common throughout the area on coral and rocky reefs from shallow water to depths of about 20m (66ft). It usually swims a few feet above the seabed, and is often seen at cleaning stations.

2 Nassau Grouper

3 Red Grouper

4 Red Hind

5 Graysby

6 Yellowfin Grouper

7 Tiger Grouper

8 CONEY
Cephalopholis fulvus

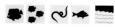

Identification of this species is complicated because it exists in three distinct colour phases: red with blue spots, half red and half white with blue spots, and brilliant yellow all over with a few blue spots on the head. The coney is a small species, growing to a length of about 41cm (1ft 4in). *Ecology*: common on rocky and coral reefs throughout the region, from shallow water to depths of about 20m (66ft). It may be gregarious, and can usually be approached fairly easily.

9 HARLEQUIN BASS
Serranus tigrinus

There are around a dozen species of small serranid referred to as 'bass', including species of the genera *Serranus* and *Liopropoma*. Most

are brightly coloured and, with the exception of the creolefish (see below), are less than 10cm (4in) long. The harlequin bass is easily recognizable by its yellow and black 'tiger' stripes. It grows to a maximum length of about 10cm (4in). *Ecology*: common in a range of habitats throughout the region from shallow water to depths of at least 40m (130ft).

10 CREOLEFISH
Paranthias furcifer

This member of the grouper family is readily recognizable by its forked tail, pinkish body with three white spots on the back, and the red spot at the base of the pectoral fin. It has a small mouth suitable for snapping up zooplankton, and grows to a maximum length of about 35cm (1ft 2in). *Ecology*: occurs throughout the region, especially on deep, steep reefs where it may form large aggregations in plankton-rich waters.

SOAPFISH
FAMILY GRAMMISTIDAE

Soapfish are grouper-like fish with large mouths and sturdy bodies. They produce a poisonous mucus that covers the skin and protects them from predators. In the confined space of an aquarium, the toxin is sufficient to kill other fish. Several species of soapfish occur in the western Atlantic, but they are fairly secretive and may be overlooked. They often hide in holes and crevices, but sometimes can be seen out in the open, leaning nonchalantly against the rocks. This is probably a ploy to put potential prey off their guard. If divers move carefully, these fish can be approached very closely, but if a potential meal comes close then the soapfish makes a sudden dash from its recumbent position.

1 GREATER SOAPFISH
Rypticus saponaceus

This species is drab in colour, with indistinct pale blotches and spots, and has a pointed head with a distinctively upturned mouth. It grows to a length of about 33cm (1ft 1in). *Ecology*: occurs on reefs from southern Florida southwards, from shallow water to depths of around 55m (180ft).

2 WHITESPOTTED SOAPFISH
Rypticus maculatus

This species is similar to the greater soapfish but is distinguished by the scattered, dark-edged white spots towards the back of the body. *Ecology*: occurs on reefs in north Florida.

8 Coney (golden phase)

9 Harlequin Bass

10 Creolefish

1 Greater Soapfish

2 Whitespotted Soapfish

HAMLETS

Hamlets are small members of the family Serranidae that occur on western Atlantic reefs, but not in the Indo-Pacific. Some believe there is only a single species, which occurs in ten different colour forms or varieties. Others split the varieties into separate species. Hamlets defend large territories during the day and are highly aggressive to competitors, such as other hamlets, that have an identical diet of small fish and invertebrates. However, they disregard territorial and aggressive herbivores such as damselfish (*Stegastes*) that are not competing for the same resource. At dusk, hamlets may leave their territories and come together in pairs to spawn.

1 BARRED HAMLET

Hypoplectrus puella

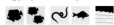

H. puella has a wide brown saddle in the middle of the body and three narrower bars behind. The head is adorned with narrow blue lines and spots. *Ecology*: common throughout the region on rocky and coral reefs from shallow water to depths of about 20m (66ft).

2 INDIGO HAMLET

Hypoplectrus indigo

The indigo hamlet has blue bars on a white body – the one in the middle is the widest. *Ecology*: common in the Cayman Islands from shallow water to depths of 40m (130ft), but mainly rare elsewhere.

3 SHY HAMLET

Hypoplectrus guttavarius

The shy hamlet has a brownish patch on its back but the rest of the body and all the fins are yellow. It has several short, bright blue lines on its head. *Ecology*: occurs throughout the area and is particularly common in the Cayman Islands, from shallow water to depths of about 30m (98ft).

BASSLETS

FAMILY *GRAMMATIDAE*

Members of the family *Grammatidae* are small, colourful fish closely related to groupers. Five species occur in the region, and they tend to be seen on deeper parts of the reef, usually around caves and recesses. They feed on planktonic crustaceans, and males have the unusual habit of brooding eggs in the mouth.

1 FAIRY BASSLET

Gramma loreto

This species is recognized by its yellow rear, purple front and dark lines through its eye. It reaches a maximum of 8cm (3in). *Ecology*: widespread on reefs of the Bahamas and Caribbean, but absent from Florida. It usually occurs in small groups close to recesses from shallow water to depths of about 60m (195ft). When inside caves the fish orientate themselves to the cave wall, so appearing to swim 'upside-down'.

2 BLACKCAP BASSLET

Gramma melacara

The purple body and black head make this an easily recognized species. It reaches a maximum length of about 10cm (4in). *Ecology*: absent from Florida and the eastern Caribbean islands, but common elsewhere. It occurs from depths of 11 to 60m (36 to 195ft) but is especially common in deeper water. Like the fairy basslet it is usually associated with caves and recesses.

1 Barred Hamlet

2 Indigo Hamlet

5 Shy Hamlet

1 Fairy Basslet

2 Blackcap Basslet

CARDINALFISH
FAMILY APOGONIDAE

Cardinalfish are small, with large eyes and mouth, and two dorsal fins. Most are pale reddish in colour with one or more dark bands or dots near the base of the tail. Over 15 species occur in the area but they are often hidden in caves during the day, emerging at night to feed on plankton. An unusual feature of cardinalfish is that the male broods eggs in his mouth until they are ready to hatch.

1 BELTED CARDINALFISH
Apogon townsendi

This species can be recognized by the dark bar running between the second dorsal and anal fin, and two narrower bars further back (these may sometimes be 'filled in' with dark colouring, making a wide bar). It reaches a maximum length of about 3.8cm (1½in). *Ecology*: occurs on reefs throughout the region, from shallow water to depths of about 50m (165ft). It is more often seen at night, when it emerges to feed. During the day it may gather in aggregations inside caves, or hide singly in holes.

2 PALE CARDINALFISH
Apogon planifrons

The pale cardinalfish has a wide bar running from the back of the second dorsal down to the anal fin, and a second narrower bar at the base of the tail. Despite its name, it may sometimes be deep orange-pink in colour. It grows to a maximum length of about 11cm (4¼in). *Ecology*: occurs on reefs throughout the region, from shallow water to depths of over 40m (130ft). It hides in caves and recesses during the day, and emerges at night to feed on plankton.

3 BIGTOOTH CARDINALFISH
Apogon affinis

This species has a pinkish to translucent body, transparent fins and a darkish bar across the eye. It grows to a length of about 10cm (4in). *Ecology*: occurs on reefs throughout the region, especially in deeper areas, down to about 40m (130ft). The bigtooth cardinalfish is fairly uncommon and more likely to be seen at night when it emerges from caves and other hiding places to feed on plankton. Like other species it is easily confused by torchlight.

HAWKFISH
FAMILY CIRRHITIDAE

1 REDSPOTTED HAWKFISH
Amblycirrhitus pinos

Hawkfish have a single dorsal fin and short tassle-like filaments projecting from the top of the dorsal spines. The lower rays of the pectoral fin are longer and thicker than the rest, and are used to help prop the fish up on the bottom. *A. pinos* is the only species occurring in the Caribbean area. It has brown and white bars on the body, is covered with tiny red spots, and grows to a length of about 10cm (4in). *Ecology*: occurs on shallow to mid-depth coral and rocky reefs throughout the region. Hawkfish have no air bladder and are poor swimmers, so tend to sit still, resting on the stout lower portion of their pectoral fins, lying in wait for small fish and crustaceans, which they ambush with skill. They are wary of divers and jump off to new vantage points when too close an approach is made.

1 Belted Cardinalfish

2 Pale Cardinalfish

3 Bigtooth Cardinalfish

1 Redspotted Hawkfish

BIGEYES
FAMILY PRIACANTHIDAE

The general body shape, large eyes and habits of these fish are similar to soldierfish, but bigeyes can be identified by their continuous dorsal fin, small scales on the body and larger eyes. By day they rest in caves, under ledges or close to coral. At night they move up and away from the reef into open water, to feed on large zooplankton. Like some other nocturnal fish, bigeyes have a reflective tapetal layer, just as cats do. This is known to almost double the amount of light absorbed.

1 GLASSEYE SNAPPER
Priacanthus cruentatus

This species has silvery bars on the body and small red spots on the dorsal, anal and tail fins. It reaches a maximum length of about 30cm (1ft). *Ecology:* occurs in warm waters throughout the world, and in the western Atlantic is seen no deeper than about 20m depth (66ft).

2 BIGEYE
Priacanthus arenatus

The Bigeye is deep reddish in colour, occasionally with dusky markings. It reaches a maximum length of about 40cm (1ft 4in). *Ecology:* occurs on reefs throughout the area, especially in deeper water.

TILEFISH
FAMILY MALACANTHIDAE

1 SAND TILEFISH
Malacanthus plumieri

Sand tilefish have an elongate body with a long, continuous dorsal fin and a long anal fin. *M. plumieri* is the only species associated with coral reefs in the area. It has a pale-coloured body with light yellow and blue markings on the head. The outer margins of the tail are usu-

ally yellow, and there is a dark blotch on the upper part of the tail. It reaches a maximum length of about 60cm (2ft). *Ecology:* occurs throughout the region in sandy and rubble areas adjacent to reefs. It is occasionally seen in shallow water but more commonly in deeper water, and may be seen down to 50m (165ft). These fish are usually seen hovering above their burrows, which they dive into if disturbed and also retreat into at night.

SNOOKS
FAMILY CENTROPOMIDAE

1 SNOOK
Centropomus undecimalis

C. undecimalis is recognised by its dark lateral line, silvery body and transparent or silvery fins. It grows to a length of about 140cm

(55in). Ecology: occurs throughout the region, but prefers coastal mangroves and so is very seldom seen around the islands of the Bahamas and eastern Caribbean. It sometimes moves onto patch reefs, usually in small groups. The snook is fairly wary of divers and generally moves away if approached.

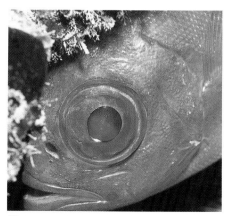

1 Glasseye Snapper

2 Bigeye

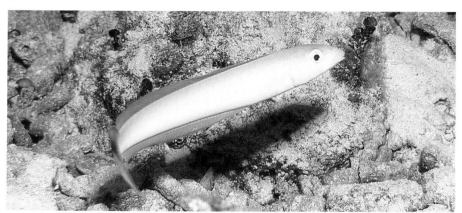

1 Sand Tilefish

1 Snook

REMORAS
FAMILY ECHENEIDAE

1 SHARKSUCKER
Echeneis naucrates

The sharksucker is easily recognizable by its highly modified spiny dorsal fin, which is formed into a long, ridged sucking disk. It reaches a length of about 1m (3ft 3in).

Ecology: *E. naucrates* occurs in tropical and warm waters around the globe. It is uniquely adapted for hitching rides on large fish, sea turtles and aquatic mammals and may even attempt to hang on to divers, but does no harm and can be easily dislodged. The sharksucker feeds on scraps of food discarded by its host, and occasionally on external parasites.

JACKS
FAMILY CARANGIDAE

Jacks are powerful swimmers that roam tropical and sub-tropical oceans but are regularly seen on reefs, particularly on seaward reefs with steep profiles. They have silvery, streamlined bodies, a narrow tail base and forked tail. Most species can be recognised by the line of bony plates called scutes, which run each side along the midline of the tail stem. Some have a single small finlet dorsally and ventrally (but not a long series of finlets as in the similarly shaped tunas). Most jacks are fish hunters, and they often patrol the reef edge in schools. They tend to have a wide geographic range and some species seen on reefs (such as the brown jack *Caranx lugubris*) occur throughout the world's tropical waters. All jacks are important food fish.

1 PALOMETA
Trachinotus goodei

The palometa is deep bodied and has very long extensions to the dorsal, anal and tail fins. These are dark in colour and there are also four thin, darkish, vertical lines on the body. This species reaches a maximum length of about 50cm (1ft 8in). *Ecology*: occurs throughout the region, although is common only in the eastern and southern Caribbean. It occurs in shallow water, especially in the surf zone, and sometimes forms large swirling shoals.

2 BIGEYE SCAD
Selar crumenophthalmus

This species is elongate with two distinct dorsal fins and a large eye. It has a yellowish stripe along each side of the body and reaches a length of about 40cm (1ft 4in). *Ecology*: the bigeye scad occurs in tropical waters around the globe and is an important fisheries species. It forms large schools, with younger fish visiting bays and shallow reefs while the larger adults tend to move into offshore waters. They feed mostly on small benthic organisms when inshore and large zooplankton when offshore.

3 BLACK JACK
Caranx lugubris

The colour of *C. lugubris* is variable, ranging from dark to light grey. The fins are usually darker and the body less silvery than in other species. It is deep bodied, and reaches a length of about 100cm (3ft 3in). *Ecology*: occurs in warm waters around the globe and turns up occasionally on outer reefs. They seem to be attracted by diver's bubbles and may make a number of passes.

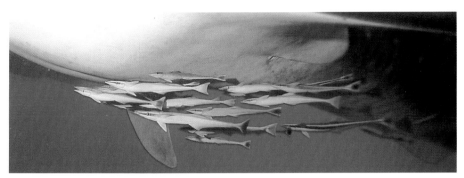

1 Sharksucker

1 Palometa

2 Bigeye Scad

3 Black Jack

4 BAR JACK
Caranx ruber

Juveniles have seven dark bars that fade as the fish develop, and the adults have a distinct bright blue and black stripe on the back, which extends on to the tail. Their entire body may suddenly darken, especially in individuals that are feeding near the seabed. The bar jack grows to a length of about 60cm (2ft). *Ecology*: occurs throughout the region and may be common in areas of rich coral growth. This gregarious jack sometimes gathers in large aggregations, but may also be seen following and mingling with bottom-feeding fish such as stingrays and goatfish. By doing this they put themselves in an ideal position to snatch up prey that has been disturbed, discarded or missed by their foraging associates. Bar jack are unafraid of divers and seem to be attracted by their bubbles.

5 HORSE-EYE JACK
Caranx latus

The distinguishing features of the horse-eye jack are its yellow tail, large eye and single small dark spot on the shoulder. It reaches a maximum length of 76cm (2ft 6in). *Ecology*: occurs in groups or shoals on offshore reefs from the surface to depths of about 30m (98ft), sometimes mixing with the crevalle jack *Caranx hippos* (distinguished by its steeply curved head and additional dark spots on the pectoral fins). Aggregations of horse-eye jack sometimes take up residence around particular reef features and are unafraid of divers.

6 YELLOW JACK
Caranx bartholomaei

Several jacks have a yellow tail, but in this species, the other fins and the belly are also yellowish. The yellow jack reaches a maximum length of about 90cm (3ft). *Ecology*: occurs throughout the region, from shallow water to depths of 40m (130ft), mainly on offshore reefs. This species is usually solitary or in small groups; it is unafraid of divers and seems to be attracted by their bubbles. It may make repeated passes above diver's heads, apparently enjoying the sensation of the exhalent stream of air.

SNAPPERS
FAMILY LUTJANIDAE

Snappers are perch-like fish with a continuous dorsal fin, a strongly or slightly forked tail, and a large mouth with well-developed canine teeth in both jaws. They are sometimes confused with grunts, which have a similar body profile but no canine teeth. Snappers tend to aggregate around reefs during the day, then move into adjacent sandy areas at night to feed on invertebrates such as crustaceans, gastropods, sea urchins, octopus and small fish.

1 YELLOWTAIL SNAPPER
Ocyurus chrysurus

The bright yellow midline and yellow tail are diagnostic of this species. It also usually has yellow spots against a bluish background on the upper part of the body. Maximum length is about 75cm (2ft 6in). *Ecology*: the yellowtail snapper is very common on shallow to mid-depth reefs throughout the region, occurring singly or in small groups. Unlike many other snappers it is active during the day, swimming fast along the reef in search of fish prey. It is unafraid of divers.

4 Bar Jack

5 Horse-eye Jack

6 Yellow Jack

1 Yellowtail Snapper

2 SCHOOLMASTER
Lutjanus apodus

The fins of this species are yellow and usually eight pale bars are visible on the upper body. There are several fine blue lines under the eye. Maximum length is about 60cm (2ft). *Ecology*: the schoolmaster is common to abundant throughout the region, occurring in a range of habitats, including mangroves, seagrass beds and reefs. It is wary of divers.

3 DOG SNAPPER
Lutjanus jocu

The dog snapper varies in colour from grey to reddish-brown and can be identified by the whitish triangular mark and narrow blue lines below the eye. This species grows to a length of about 90cm (3ft). *Ecology*: occurs close to rock and coral reefs and wrecks throughout the region. It is generally found at depths of 10 to 30m (33 to 98ft). The dog snapper is a very shy species, which always keeps its distance.

4 GRAY SNAPPER
Lutjanus griseus

This species varies in colour from greyish to a reddish bronze. It may have a dark stripe through the eye, indistinct bars on the body and a dusky margin to the tail fin. The gray snapper grows to a length of about 60cm (2ft). *Ecology*: occurs throughout the region in a range of habitats, including mangroves, rocky areas and inshore coral reefs. It usually gathers in small groups and is unafraid of divers.

GRUNTS
FAMILY HAEMULIDAE

Grunts are medium- to large-sized fish that look quite similar to snappers, but differ by having smaller teeth and by having one set located in the throat. It is these pharyngeal teeth that give the group their name. When ground together they produce a sound that is then amplified by the swim bladder so that it becomes an audible grunt.

Juvenile grunts spend most of their time among seagrass where they feed on plankton. Most are whitish-silver with darker, longitudinal markings and a dot on the tail base. They are difficult to identify at this stage. Adult grunts are relatively inactive during the day. They generally gather in groups and hang almost motionless in the shelter of the reef. Most grunts are quite wary and need to be approached quietly and slowly. Occasionally they can be seen 'kissing'. This is not friendship, but mouth-to-mouth combat associated with territorial display. At night, grunts move to nearby sandy areas and seagrass beds where they hunt for crustaceans. Often their nocturnal colour patterns are different – for example they may lose the bright stripes and become more blotchy. There are about 17 species of grunt in the western Atlantic region.

3 PORKFISH
Anisotremus virginicus

The porkfish is identified by the black diagonal bars and yellow stripes on the body. The juvenile has a yellow head, two longitudinal black stripes and a black spot on the tail base. It reaches a length of about 40cm (1ft 4in). *Ecology*: common in Florida, where it forms large schools around rocks and reefs at depths of 2 to 20m (6 to 66ft). It is much less numerous in the Caribbean, Bahamas and Bermuda, occurring only singly or in small groups. Adults feed mainly on hard-shelled invertebrates; juveniles act as cleaners, picking parasites off other fish.

2 Schoolmaster

3 Dog Snapper

4 Gray Snapper

1 Porkfish

2 FRENCH GRUNT
Haemulon flavolineatum

This species is distinguished by its broad yellow stripes and yellow fins. The stripes above the lateral line are horizontal, those below slope obliquely. It grows to a length of about 30cm (12in). *Ecology*: juvenile French grunt are often abundant in nearshore seagrass beds, while the adult occurs on reefs from shallow water to depths of about 20m (66ft), especially around large coral and rock features. Every evening, they move off the reef along well-swum paths, heading for nearby seagrass beds, where they hunt out crustaceans. *H. flavolineatum* is one of the commonest grunts in the region and, although sometimes seen singly, more often gathers in aggregations consisting of hundreds or even thousands of individuals. French grunts often form the nucleus of mixed-species schools, which include yellow goatfish (*Mulloidichthys martinicus*), white grunt (*Haemulon plumieri*) and various snappers. These species do not compete with each other, and gathering together provides safety in numbers.

3 SMALLMOUTH GRUNT
Haemulon chrysargyreum

This species can be confused with the striped grunt *H. striatum*, but the latter has silvery to whitish fins, brownish-yellow stripes and no stripes on the belly. The smallmouth grunt has yellow lines and yellow fins. It grows to a length of about 23cm (9in). *Ecology*: occurs throughout the region where it forms small aggregations around rocks and reefs from depths of approximately 2 to 18m (6 to 59ft). Often found in the vicinity of elkhorn or staghorn coral, it has a mixed diet of plankton, polychaete worms and small crustaceans. Individuals of this species, like several others, are rather wary of divers and tend to move away unless a very careful approach is made.

4 BLUESTRIPED GRUNT
Haemulon sciurus

This species is recognizable by the numerous blue stripes along the body and the dusky dorsal and tail fin. The white grunt *Haemulon plumieri* is similar, but the blue lines on this species occur only on the head. *H. sciurus* grows to a length of about 45cm (1ft 6in). *Ecology*: common throughout the region, usually in small aggregations near reefs, rocks and drop-offs, from depths of 4 to 20m (13 to 66ft). It feeds mainly on crustaceans, bivalves and other shelled animals.

5 COTTONWICK
Haemulon melanurum

The cottonwick is distinguished by the dark dorsal fin, dark line on top of the body extending on to the tail, thin dark line from mouth to eye and yellow lines on the body. It grows to a length of about 33cm (1ft 1in). *Ecology*: occurs throughout the region, but is generally uncommon. It is usually in small groups close to reefs in clear water, from depths of 3 to 20m (10 to 66ft), with juveniles generally in deeper water of 30m (98ft).

6 WHITE MARGATE
Haemulon album

This species has a dusky tail and soft dorsal, and may have three feint stripes along the body, but otherwise is fairly uniformly grey. It is the largest species in the genus, growing to a length of about 60cm (2ft). *Ecology*: occurs throughout the region and is found in a range of habitats at depths of 2 to 15m (6 to 49ft), including seagrass beds, sandy areas, rock and coral reefs. Usually alone or in small groups, the white margate feeds by day and night on bottom-dwelling invertebrates such as heart urchins, which it hunts for in the sand. Like other grunts, this nocturnal foraging may produce 'halos' of disturbed seabed around patch reefs.

2 French Grunt

3 Smallmouth Grunt

4 Bluestriped Grunt

5 Cottonwick

6 White Margate

PORGIES
FAMILY SPARIDAE

Porgies are in the bream family, which also has many representatives in temperate seas. They are silvery snapper-like fish with a deep body, steep head profile and single dorsal fin. The mouth is terminal but set low down, well below the level of the eyes. There are a number of similar species, and underwater identification can be difficult. Porgies feed on hard-shelled invertebrates, particularly in sandy and rubble areas adjacent to reefs. Most are solitary.

1 PLUMA
Calamus pennatula

The pluma is yellowish in colour with numerous thin blue lines on the head. It reaches a maximum length of 38cm (1ft 3in). *Ecology*: absent from Florida, where it is replaced by two other very similar species. Occurs elsewhere in the region from shallow water to depths of over 80m (260ft). It is especially common in the Bahamas and eastern Caribbean.

2 SHEEPSHEAD PORGY
Calamus penna

  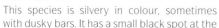

This species is silvery in colour, sometimes with dusky bars. It has a small black spot at the axil of the pectoral fin, vertical white marks on the head and reaches a maximum length of 46cm (1ft 6in). *Ecology*: occurs throughout the region in sandy habitats adjacent to reefs.

3 SAUCEREYE PORGY
Calamus calamus

This species gets its name from the large eye, which has a bluish line below it. The body colour is silvery with a bluish or yellowish tinge but it can change rapidly and may become blotchy or striped. It reaches a maximum length of about 40cm (1ft 4in). *Ecology*: occurs throughout the region in sandy habitats adjacent to reefs, from shallow water to depths of around 70m (230ft).

DRUMS
FAMILY SCIAENIDAE

1 SPOTTED DRUM
Equetus punctatus

These fish get their name from the drumming sound that they produce, which is caused by the vibration of special muscles that are attached to, or run close to, the swimbladder. The muscles contract and expand at a very fast rate of about 24 contractions per second, causing the walls of the swimbladder to vibrate. The vibrations are then amplified by the bladder to produce the drumming. The spotted drum has a distinctive, very high front dorsal fin, black and white bars on the head and spots towards the rear end of the body and on the tail. The juvenile has even more pronounced fins but lacks the black spots. It reaches a maximum length of about 28cm (11in). *Ecology*: occurs throughout the region, from shallow water to depths of about 30m (98ft). It is unafraid of divers but is a fairly secretive fish, generally hiding during the day under ledges or close to the entrance of small caves. It comes out at night to feed on small invertebrates.

1 Pluma

2 Sheepshead Porgy

3 Saucereye Porgy

1 Spotted Drum (Juvenile)

1 Spotted Drum (Adult)

GOATFISH
FAMILY MULLIDAE

Goatfish have two barbels under the chin, which may be tucked neatly away between the lower parts of the gill cover when not in use. Although goatfish are sometimes seen around reefs, most are associated with sandy habitats, where they use the barbels to hunt out small buried organisms. The barbels move independently and bear numerous sense organs. Once prey such as crustaceans and molluscs have been located they are either 'excavated' or blown out of the sand, so that they can be captured.

1 YELLOW GOATFISH
Mulloidichthys martinicus

This species has a white body with yellow fins and a yellow stripe along the midline. It reaches a maximum length of 40cm (1ft 4in). *Ecology*: common in sandy and rubble areas, from shallow water to depths of about 40m (130ft). It feeds alone or in small groups and sometimes forms large aggregations.

2 SPOTTED GOATFISH
Pseudupeneus maculatus

When feeding this species has three dark spots along the midline, but when the fish is resting on the bottom, the body becomes mottled to blend in with its surroundings. It reaches a maximum length of 28cm (11in). *Ecology*: occurs in sandy and rubble areas throughout the region, from shallow water to depths of about 12m (39ft).

SWEEPERS
FAMILY PEMPHERIDAE

1 GLASSY SWEEPER
Pempheris schomburgki

Sweepers have deep bodies, a continuous dorsal fin and very large eyes. The glassy sweeper is coppery in colour with a dark band along the base of the anal fin. It reaches a maximum length of about 15cm (6in). *Ecology*: occurs throughout the region, from depths of 3 to 30m (10 to 98ft). During the day it gathers in groups or schools that drift back and forth in caves and other sheltered, shady places. It emerges at night to feed on zooplankton.

CHUB
FAMILY KYPHOSIDAE

Chub (sometimes called rudderfish) have a relatively deep body with a continuous dorsal fin. The head is pointed and the mouth relatively small.

1 BERMUDA CHUB
Kyphosus sectatrix

K. sectatrix has a silvery body with yellow lines and a white and brown mark under the eye. It reaches a length of about 40cm (1ft 4in). *Ecology*: occurs around rocky and coral reefs, from very shallow water to depths of about 30m (98ft). It usually occurs in groups and sometimes forms large aggregations. It feeds on algal debris and attached plants.

1 Yellow Goatfish

2 Spotted Goatfish

1 Glassy Sweeper

1 Bermuda Chub

SPADEFISH
FAMILY EPHIPPIDAE

1 ATLANTIC SPADEFISH
Chaetodipterus faber

The spadefish has a deep, highly compressed body with a small mouth and high dorsal and anal fins. It is silvery, with at least five dark bars on the head and body, and dark margins to the fins. These markings tend to disappear with age and may also suddenly fade dramatically depending on the fish's behaviour, but this species can always be recognized by its unusual body shape. It reaches a maximum length of about 90cm (3ft). *Ecology*: occurs throughout the area, from shallow water to depths of about 25m (82ft). Adults congregate in groups or schools above reefs and wrecks and are unafraid of divers. Juveniles inhabit seagrass beds and sandy areas. They are darker in colour and mimic mangrove leaves, drifting gently back and forth on their sides in shallow water.

BUTTERFLYFISH
FAMILY CHAETODONTIDAE

Butterflyfish have an extremely compressed and fairly deep body with a small terminal mouth and fine brush-like teeth. They have perfected the art of masking the eyes with a dark stripe in order to confuse potential predators. Eyebars conceal the location of the real eyes, which are thought to be used as 'targets' by predatory fish. Butterflyfish move around the reef during the day, either singly or in pairs, and most have a territory or home range that they defend. They often occur in heterosexual pairs, and the pairs may remain together for several years – sometimes for life. At night they retreat to safe places among rocks and coral and many adopt a different colour pattern. Butterflyfish feed on a range of small food items, including coral polyps, the tube feet of sea urchins, small crabs and filamentous algae.

1 FOUREYE BUTTERFLYFISH
Chaetodon capistratus

An ocellus or eye spot is present at the rear of the body at all stages in the growth of this species. The juvenile has an additional smaller ocellus above the large one and has two dark bars on the body, plus one on the head. The adult has only a single dark bar, masking the real eye; the rest of the body is greyish with numerous fine lines radiating in a chevron pattern from the midline. This species reaches a length of about 16cm (6in). *Ecology*: this is the commonest butterflyfish in the region, occurring on coral reefs from shallow water to depths of about 20m (66ft). It usually moves around in pairs, feeding on a range of attached animals such as gorgonians, zoanthids, ascidians and polychaete worms.

2 BANDED BUTTERFLYFISH
Chaetodon striatus

The juvenile of this species is similar to *C. capistratus*, but lacks the large ocellus and instead has two dark bars on the tail and an ocellus on the soft dorsal. The latter fades as the fish develops, and is absent in the adult. The adult is easily distinguished by the two wide dark bars on the body. This species reaches a length of about 16cm (6¼in). *Ecology*: occurs on coral reefs throughout the region, from shallow water to depths of about 20m (66ft). It is also found along the east coast of the United States, as far north as Massachusetts, due to transport of larvae on the warm Gulf Stream currents. It may be single or in pairs and feeds on coral polyps, crustaceans and polychaete worms.

1 Atlantic Spadefish

1 Foureye Butterflyfish

2 Banded Butterflyfish

3 SPOTFIN BUTTERFLYFISH
Chaetodon ocellatus

This species gets its name from the small black spot on the top of the soft dorsal fin. It has a dark bar through the eye, the fins are bright yellow and the body whitish. It grows to a maximum length of about 20cm (8in). *Ecology*: occurs on coral reefs throughout the region, from shallow water to depths of about 20m (66ft). Particularly common in Florida, and occasionally larvae are carried in the Gulf Stream up the East coast. The spotfin may be single or in pairs and has a mixed diet of small benthic organisms.

4 LONGSNOUT BUTTERFLYFISH
Chaetodon aculeatus

As its name suggests, this species has an unusually long snout. It lacks a dark bar through the eye, but has a brownish saddle at the back of the body. The maximum length of the longsnout butterflyfish is about 9cm (3½in). *Ecology*: occurs on coral reefs throughout the region, from shallow water to depths of about 90m (295ft). It is usually solitary and is very shy, darting rapidly into the shelter of recesses if disturbed. It feeds on the tubefeet of sea urchins, polychaete worm tentacles and other small invertebrates.

ANGELFISH
FAMILY *POMACANTHIDAE*

Angelfish are superficially similar to butterflyfish, but can readily be distinguished by the prominent spine on the edge of the gill cover. They are important browsers on attached life. In the western Atlantic, the three common species (rock beauty, gray angelfish and French angelfish) have diets consisting of algae and numerous species of sponge. In addition, the gray and French angelfish feed on gorgonians. Juvenile French angels also act as 'cleaners', removing external parasites and bits of debris from other reef fish.

Angelfish are hermaphrodites, functioning first as females, then as males. Most are territorial and live in 'harems' consisting of a single male with several females. The size of the territory ranges from a few square metres to over a thousand square metres.

1 GRAY ANGELFISH
Pomacanthus arcuatus

The adult is the least colourful of the Caribbean angelfish, being an overall grey with white around the mouth. The juvenile has five yellow bars on a black background and is very similar to the juvenile French angelfish. It can be distinguished by the truncated tail fin and narrrow black band with a broad pale margin. *P. arcuatus* reaches a maximum length of about 60cm (2ft). *Ecology*: very common and widely distributed on reefs throughout the region, from shallow water to depths of about 30m (98ft). This species is inquisitive and friendly towards divers, providing excellent photo opportunities.

2 FRENCH ANGELFISH
Pomacanthus paru

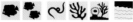

The yellow-edged scales of the adult are distinctive. The juvenile with its black and yellow bars is sometimes confused with the juvenile of the gray angelfish, but can be identified by the rounded tail fin with its wider black band and narrow yellow margin. The French angelfish is one of the largest angelfish in the western Atlantic, reaching a length of about 46cm (1½ft). *Ecology*: fairly common throughout the region, occurring on coral reefs from shallow water to depths of about 100m (330ft). French angelfish generally move around in pairs and do not mind being approached by divers.

3 Spotfin Butterflyfish

4 Longsnout Butterflyfish

2 French Angelfish (Juvenile)

1 Gray Angelfish

2 French Angelfish (Adult)

3 ROCK BEAUTY
Holacanthus tricolor

The bright yellow and black colouration of the adult is very distinct. The juvenile is bright yellow with a blue-ringed, black ocellus on the back, and closely resembles the juvenile three-spot damselfish, *Stegastes planifrons*. The rock beauty grows to a length of about 30cm (1ft). *Ecology*: occurs on reefs throughout the region from shallow water to depths of about 90m (295ft). Males typically defend a large territory that includes smaller territories of two to four females.

4 QUEEN ANGELFISH
Holacanthus ciliaris

The blue-rimmed 'crown' on the forehead of the adult, blue lips and yellow tail is very distinctive. The juvenile is quite different, with a dark blue-edged bar through the eye and two or more bright blue lines on the body. These lines are curved, in contrast to the otherwise identical juvenile of the blue angelfish *H. bermudensis*, in which the lines are straight in the middle. *Ecology*: occurs on reefs throughout the region from depths of 6 to 18m (20–59ft). This species is either solitary or lives in pairs, and is fairly shy.

DAMSELFISH
FAMILY POMACENTRIDAE

Members of this family are likely to be seen on most dives. There are 14 species in the region, and another two that occur only in Brazil. Pomacentrids are small fish, with oval to elongate bodies and a small terminal mouth. Many of the adults are drab in colour, but juveniles are often a bright combination of yellow and blue. Some damselfish feed on plankton, and typically form aggregations in mid-water. Others are omnivores or herbivores and stay close to the bottom. These species are territorial and some are so aggressive that they will readily take on divers who intrude on to their patch.

1 THREESPOT DAMSELFISH
Stegastes planifrons

This is one of the commonest of the six species of *Stegastes* occurring in the Caribbean. The adult is yellowish-grey, becoming duskier with age. It is identified by the bright yellow mark above the eye and dark spot at the base of the pectoral fin and upper tail stem. Juveniles are golden yellow with a dark spot on the tail base and another on the back. Its maximum length is about 12.5cm (5in). *Ecology*: inshore and offshore reefs throughout the region, including Bermuda, especially in areas of rich algal growth. Threespot damselfish cultivate and protect their algal 'lawn', removing unwanted growths and chasing off intruders and competitors, by making sounds and biting. Divers as well as fish are attacked by this pugnacious species.

2 BEAUGREGORY
Stegastes leucostictus

Colour is variable in this species, ranging from yellowish-blue to dusky brown and becoming darker with age. Juveniles are yellow with a blue back. Both adults and juveniles are similar to *Stegastes variabilis*, but the latter species has a distinctive black spot on the upper tail stem. The beaugregory reaches a maximum length of about 10cm (4in). *Ecology*: occurs throughout the region, including Bermuda. It is found in a range of habitats, including coral and rocky reefs, seagrass beds and sandy areas, from very shallow water to depths of 10m (33ft). Defends a territory, but is less aggressive than other species and allows divers to approach quite close.

3 Rock Beauty

4 Queen Angelfish

1 Threespot Damselfish (Juvenile)

1 Threespot Damselfish (Adult)

2 Beaugregory

4 BICOLOR DAMSELFISH
Stegastes partitus

This species is easily identified by its dark front and light-coloured rear. Individuals living in deeper water may have dark caudal, dorsal and anal fins. This species reaches a maximum length of about 10cm (4in). *Ecology*: common throughout the region, including Bermuda, from shallow water to 45m (150ft). It occurs on shallow reefs and seagrass beds, and also on isolated patch reefs in deeper water. The bicolor damselfish aggressively defends a small territory but does not attempt to drive away large fish, or divers.

4 YELLOWTAIL DAMSELFISH
Microspathodon chrysurus

The characteristic feature of this species is its yellow tail. This is also seen in the intermediate-sized fish, but juveniles, up to 8cm (3in), have a whitish tail. These small individuals (often referred to as jewelfish) have a blue body with many paler blue spots. As the fish grows the body becomes darker and the spots fewer in number. It reaches a maximum length of about 19cm (7½in). *Ecology*: found on coral reefs throughout the area, including Bermuda, from shallow water to depths of about 15m (49ft). Juveniles hide among branching fire coral *Millepora*, and are very wary of divers. They remove external parasites from other fish, and also feed on coral polyps and small invertebrates. Adults maintain small territories and feed on algae – they are bold and unafraid.

5 SERGEANT MAJOR
Abudefduf saxatilis

The amount of yellow on the sergeant major varies, but the five dark bars are distinctive. When nesting, the male becomes dark blue. This species reaches a length of about 18cm (7in). One other *Abudefduf* species occurs in the region but it is much less common, lives close to the bottom and its five dark bars are

wider and brownish in colour. *Ecology*: the sergeant major is abundant throughout the region, including Bermuda. Juveniles may be seen in rock pools or taking refuge in floating sargassum weed, but adults gather in aggregations above coral and rocky reefs, where they feed on plankton. They may indulge in mass spawning, where a group of fish moves along the reef, the males 'dropping-out' on to selected nest sites as they go.

6 BLUE CHROMIS
Chromis cyanea

Chromis species are distinguished from other pomacentrids by their slender bodies and forked tails. The blue colour of this species separates it from the brown chromis. It reaches a length of about 13cm (5in). *Ecology*: common throughout the area, occurring on outer reef slopes and patch reefs from depths of 3 to 55m (10 to 180ft). It usually gathers in large aggregations in mid-water, where it feeds on zooplankton and often mixes with the brown chromis. Another three species of *Chromis* occur in the area, but these live in small groups, close to the bottom. Blue chromis retreat each night into the same hiding place to sleep. They also dart into this hole during the day if threatened by predators. Male blue chromis have permanent territories around this bolt-hole, and make the nest close by.

7 BROWN CHROMIS
Chromis multilineata

The brown chromis is easily recognized by its shape, brownish colour and dark spot at the base of the pectoral fin. It reaches a length of about 16.5cm (6½in). *Ecology*: occurs throughout the region, on steep slopes and patch reefs from depths of 2 to 40m (6 to 130ft). It often forms mixed aggregations with the blue chromis, and both species blend well with the bluish colour of open water. Brown chromis do not have specific holes that they retire into and are apparently more vulnerable to predation because of this.

3 Bicolor Damselfish

4 Yellowtail Damselfish

6 Blue Chromis

5 Sergeant Major

7 Brown Chromis

WRASSE
FAMILY LABRIDAE

Wrasse are a very diverse group in terms of their range of size and form. They typically have a terminal mouth with well-developed lips and one or more pairs of protruding canine teeth. Most species feed mainly on bottom-dwelling invertebrates, especially shelled animals such as molluscs, crabs and sea urchins. Special crushing teeth at the back of the throat (pharyngeal teeth) enable wrasse to deal with hard and spiky food with ease. *Thalassoma* species together with juveniles of other wrasse are well known as cleaners, feeding on crustacean ectoparasites of other reef fish.

Wrasse have what has been described as a 'flexible' mating system. In particular, it makes allowances for differences in population density, and ensures that spawning is likely to be successful under various circumstances. Most wrasse species begin their reproductive lives in a straightforward way, with females and 'initial phase' males, both of which have developed directly from juveniles. At this stage, the sexes are not easily distinguished on appearance alone, although their behaviour may give them away. Subsequently, some of the females develop into 'terminal phase' males, which are colourful, larger and more territorial than initial phase males. These fish are usually territorial, and maintain a 'harem' of females.

1 SPANISH HOGFISH
Bodianus rufus

The Spanish hogfish has a purplish upper body with yellow below, but this pattern is variable, and large adults may become mottled. The juvenile also has purple or blue on the head, but this recedes as the fish grows. The Spanish hogfish reaches a length of about 60cm (2ft). *Ecology*: occurs on rocky and coral reefs throughout the region from shallow water to depths of about 60m (195ft). It ranges widely in search of benthic animals such as crustaceans, molluscs and echinoderms. Juveniles act as cleaners.

2 HOGFISH
Lachnolaimus maximus

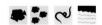

This species varies from pale to reddish brown, with the front of the head darker than the rest. It is a deep-bodied fish with a distinctly pointed snout, concave head profile and long spines at the front of the first dorsal fin. It grows to a length of about 90cm (3ft). *Ecology*: occurs on rocky and coral reefs and in sandy and rubble habitats throughout the region, from shallow water to depths of about 30m (98ft). It covers wide areas during its search for crustaceans, molluscs and sea urchins that it digs out of the sand.

3 CREOLE WRASSE
Clepticus parrae

The Creole wrasse is bluish-purple with a distinctive dark area above the eye. Juveniles are a similar colour but have dark spots and indistinct bars on the back. It grows to a maximum length of about 30cm (1ft). *Ecology*: common throughout the region, especially around deep outer reefs at depths up to 40m (130ft). In contrast with other species of wrasse in the area, it gathers in small to large aggregations several feet above the reef, where it feeds on zooplankton in open water. At night it retires to the safety of the reef.

4 GREEN RAZORFISH
Xyrichtys splendens

This species is variable but generally greenish in colour. It has a distinctive dark spot in the middle of the body, and grows to a length of about 15cm (6in). *Ecology*: occurs in sandy and seagrass habitats throughout the region, at depths down to about 15m (49ft). It has a high, narrow forehead, which is thought to be an adaptation for plunging headfirst into the sand. They do this when alarmed, then partially emerge and remain motionless with the head just showing. Razorfish feed on benthic invertebrates.

1 Spanish Hogfish

2 Hogfish (and Bar Jack)

3 Creole Wrasse

4 Green Razorfish

5 BLUEHEAD WRASSE
Thalassoma bifasciatum

The terminal phase male has a blue head followed by two dark bars separated by a white one. The rear end of the body is greenish. Initial phase males and females have alternating dark and pale bars, while the juvenile is yellow with brown marks on the head. The bluehead wrasse grows to a length of about 18cm (7in). *Ecology*: very common in a wide range of reef habitats and also on seagrass beds. It occurs throughout the region from shallow water to depths of about 40m (130ft). This species ranges widely in search of invertebrate prey, and juveniles act as cleaners, removing parasites and bits of debris from other fish.

6 PUDDING WIFE
Halichoeres radiatus

The terminal male pudding wife (also known as the supermale) is greenish to bluish, sometimes with a pale bar in the middle of the body. The smaller male fish are also greenish, but have five whitish blotches on the top of the back. The juvenile is yellowish with three dark spots on the back. The pudding wife grows to a length of about 50cm (1ft 8in). *Ecology*: common on rocky and coral reefs throughout the region from shallow water to depths of about 55m (180ft). It has a large home range which it constantly explores in search of benthic animals such as crustaceans, molluscs and echinoderms. It is a fairly timid species.

PARROTFISH
FAMILY SCARIDAE

Parrotfish are named after their teeth, which are fused into a very obvious, beak-like structure. They use this when grazing on algae or biting at corals. Many species are associated with the shallow reef habitats and their grazing activities are incessant and often noisy. In addition, they leave visible scars on the reef limestone and on living corals. They are very important producers of sand, which comes from limestone that has been ground up in the guts and then passed out.

Parrotfish, like wrasse, are hermaphrodites that function first as females, then as males. Sex changes are often accompanied by radical changes in colour, with the most gaudy individuals being the mature, terminal phase males. Parrotfish often occur in mixed-species groups that range widely over the reef during the day in their search for food. A few are territorial. All retire at night to hiding places under rocks and corals, and some species secrete a mucus cocoon that throws predators off the scent.

1 BLUE PARROTFISH
Scarus coeruleus

Juveniles and subadults are bluish with a yellow patch on the top of the head. Terminal males lose the yellow markings but can be recognized by the humped forehead. This species grows to a maximum length of about 1.2m (4ft). *Ecology*: occurs around coral reefs throughout the region (except the Gulf of Mexico), from shallow water to depths of about 25m (82ft).

2 RAINBOW PARROTFISH
Scarus guacamaia

The bright green rear of the terminal phase male is distinctive. Females and intermediate phases are similar but generally paler overall. The rainbow parrotfish grows to a maximum length of about 1.2m (4ft). *Ecology*: occurs on rocky and coral reefs throughout the area (except the Gulf of Mexico) from shallow water to depths of about 25m (82ft).

5 Bluehead Wrasse (male and female)

6 Pudding Wife

1 Blue Parrotfish

2 Rainbow Parrotfish

3 PRINCESS PARROTFISH
Scarus taeniopterus

This is one of several species that is greenish in colour with blue lines around the eye. The terminal male can be identified by the orange-yellow streak down the flank. It grows to a maximum length of about 35cm (1ft 2in). The juvenile has several brown and white horizontal stripes along the body. *Ecology*: occurs on rocky and coral reefs throughout the area from shallow water to depths of about 25m (82ft). This species builds itself a protective mucus cocoon at night.

4 STRIPED PARROTFISH
Scarus iserti

Both the adults and juvenile colouration are similar to the respective developmental stages of the princess parrotfish. The main difference is that the terminal male of the striped parrotfish has fine pink, horizontal lines on the tail fin, and an indistinct pale streak down the flank (rather than the orange one of the princess parrotfish). The striped parrotfish reaches a maximum length of about 35cm (1ft 2in). *Ecology*: occurs on rocky and coral reefs throughout the area from shallow water to depths of about 25m (82ft). In some areas it forms large feeding aggregations consisting of a few terminal males with large numbers of females. These groups can have a significant impact as they swarm along, browsing on algae and at the same time eroding the reef beneath with their scraping teeth. This species is also known to gather in big spawning aggregations on outer reefs.

5 QUEEN PARROTFISH
Scarus vetula

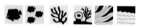

This species is also greenish in colour with blue lines around the eye. The terminal male can be identified by a light-coloured bar running along the length of the pectoral fin. It grows to a maximum length of about 60cm (2ft). The female is darkish brown with a broad white streak along the flank. *Ecology*: occurs on rocky and coral reefs throughout the region from shallow water to depths of about 25m (82ft). The queen parrotfish is well known for producing a nocturnal mucus envelope. The covering starts at the head end, and then gradually extends backwards until the whole body is enveloped. A small hole is left by the mouth. This has a flap of mucus in it which moves back and forth as the fish breathes. There is another hole by the gills, where the water exits.

6 STOPLIGHT PARROTFISH
Sparisoma viride

The stoplight parrotfish gets its name from the orange-yellow spot at the base of the tail of the terminal phase male. There is also a distinctive yellow crescent at the end of the tail, and a small yellow spot at the base of the pectoral fin. It grows to a maximum length of about 60cm (2ft). The female and juvenile are completely different – essentially darkish red-brown with white markings. *Ecology*: occurs throughout the area on rocky and coral reefs and occasionally on seagrass beds. It is found to depths of 49m (160ft).

7 REDBAND PARROTFISH
Sparisoma aurofrenatum

The terminal male of the redband parrotfish can be distinguished by the narrow red bar running across the head and the reddish anal and dorsal fins. The female has red fins and a darkish body. This species also shows rapid colour changes, often becoming mottled to blend in with the background when predators are in the vicinity. It has even been seen to mimic sea whips by hanging vertically amongst them and developing two black stripes as extra disguise. It grows to a maximum length of about 28cm (11in). *Ecology*: occurs on rocky and coral reefs throughout the area from shallow water to depths of about 20m (66ft).

3 Princess Parrotfish (Juvenile)

3 Princess Parrotfish (adult)

4 Striped Parrotfish

5 Queen Parrotfish

6 Stoplight Parrotfish

7 Redband Parrotfish

JAWFISH
FAMILY OPISTOGNATHIDAE

These are small fish with a narrow body and long, continuous dorsal fin. The mouth is large and the jaws are strong with a wide gape. Occasionally the mouth is seen stuffed with eggs, which the males incubate until they are ready to hatch. Jawfish construct burrows in the sand that they may reinforce with small stones and fragments of shell. They hover vertically above these when feeding on zooplankton, but if disturbed, rapidly retreat into the burrow tail-first, leaving just the head showing. Several species occur in the area, but they are not always easy to identify underwater.

1 YELLOWHEAD JAWFISH
Opistognathus aurifrons

This species is fairly easily identified by its yellowish head and pale body, and the fins often have a bluish tinge. It grows to a length of about 10cm (4in). *Ecology*: the yellowhead jawfish is common throughout the region. It occurs in sandy and rubble habitats adjacent to reefs, from shallow water to depths of about 40m (130ft).

2 BANDED JAWFISH
Opistognathus macrognathus

The banded jawfish has a series of darkish marks along the side of the body, and a dark spot towards the front of the dorsal fin, but these features are not visible if the fish is in its hole. It grows to a maximum length of about 20cm (8in). *Ecology*: occurs throughout the region in sandy and rubble habitats adjacent to reefs, from shallow water to depths of about 12m (39ft).

BARRACUDA
FAMILY SPHYRAENIDAE

1 GREAT BARRACUDA
Sphyraena barracuda

Barracuda are distinctive fish with elongate bodies, two widely separated dorsal fins and a forked tail. The head is pointed and the mouth large with a projecting lower jaw and long, sharp teeth. The great barracuda is easily distinguished from the other common species (such as the southern sennet *Sphyraena picudilla*) by the scattered dark markings along the body. The great barracuda is also much larger, reaching a length of about 1.8m (6ft). *Ecology*: widespread in all tropical seas and is common throughout the western Atlantic region. It may be seen in a wide range of habitats from shallow bays to open sea and reef, and has been reported at depths of 100m (330ft). Barracudas are active hunters, but, unlike many other predatory fish, do not have a protrusible upper jaw with which to suck in their prey. Neither can they open their jaws very wide to swallow large fish whole because they are fused together rather than being hinged. Instead, they rely on biting, and make full use of their impressive armoury of teeth. Often they will bite their prey into several pieces, circling back to snap them all up in a few mouthfuls. The great barracuda is interested in divers but the only circumstance when they might attack is if people are spearfishing or carrying a shiny object which attracts them.

1 Yellowhead Jawfish

2 Banded Jawfish

1 Great Barracuda

TRIPLEFINS
FAMILY TRIPTERYGIIDAE

1 ROUGHHEAD TRIPLEFIN
Enneanectes boehlkei

These blenny-like fish are readily identified by the three, separate dorsal fins. No other coral reef species have this feature. They are small fish, not exceeding about 4cm (1 ½in) in length. There are several species of triplefin, but they are very difficult to distinguish from each other underwater. *Ecology:* like other triplefins, the roughhead tends to perch on sponges or corals, blending effectively into the background. It feeds on small invertebrates.

BLENNIES
FAMILIES CLINIDAE and BLENNIDAE

Blennies are small fish. Those listed here reach a maximum length of about 6cm (2½in) unless otherwise stated. They have a single dorsal fin which in some species has a slight notch in it. Most species have scales on the body. They all tend to rest on the bottom and remain quite still, unless disturbed, when they move quickly away. Their main food is small invertebrate animals.

1 DIAMOND BLENNY
Malacoctenus boehlkei

This species has a yellowish head and normally a black spot at the front of the dorsal fin. *Ecology:* absent from Florida, but occurs elsewhere in the region from shallow water to depths of about 24m (79ft). It is usually associated with the anemone *Condylactis gigantea*.

2 SADDLED BLENNY
Malacoctenus triangulatus

The five brownish saddles along the back of this species are distinctive. The body is pale with tiny red dots. *Ecology:* common throughout the region, from shallow water to depths of about 15m (49ft).

3 SAILFIN BLENNY
Emblemaria pandionis

The male of this species can be identified if it emerges from its burrow, because it generally flicks up its greatly enlarged dorsal fin. Observ-ing this behaviour requires patience. *Ecology:* the sailfin blenny occurs throughout the region in sandy and rubble areas in shallow, clear water areas such as channels. It usually inhabits empty worm or shell holes and retreats rapidly if disturbed.

4 SPINYHEAD BLENNY
Acanthemblemaria spinosa

The spinyhead blenny has a dark head marked with white flecks, and large, protruding eyes. *Ecology:* occurs on reefs throughout the region, to depths of about 18m (59ft). It lives in small holes and darts out at intervals to catch food.

5 ROUGHHEAD BLENNY
Acanthemblemaria aspera

The body colour of this blenny varies from yellow to brownish and it is usually marked with white specks. There is a characteristic tuft of densely branched cirri on the head, just above the eyes. *Ecology:* lives in small holes in the reef, to depths of about 15m (49ft), with only the head visible. It is a fairly rare species.

1 Roughhead Triplefin

1 Diamond Blenny

2 Saddled Blenny

3 Sailfin Blenny

4 Spinyhead Blenny

5 Roughhead Blenny

SECRETARY BLENNY
Acanthemblemaria maria

The secretary blenny has a darkish head with a distinctive white streak behind the eye. The body is essentially dark, but has white specks and five or six pale bars. There is a branched tentacle above each eye (there are other species in this genus which have similar head tentacles). It grows to a maximum length of about 5cm (2in). Ecology. Like many other blennies, this species inhabits small holes such as abandoned worm tubes, from which it darts out to catch food. It is absent from Florida but seen elsewhere throughout the region, generally on shallow rocky and coral reefs.

7 ARROW BLENNY
Lucayablennius zingaro

This species is easily recognizable by its shape, colour and habits. It has an elongate body that is reddish in colour with several black spots towards the rear end. *Ecology*: the arrow blenny spends most of its time drifting out in the open, just above the surface of the reef. Its tail is held in a curled up position, ready to be rapidly straightened so that the blenny can shoot itself forward like an arrow to catch small fish. At times, it may return to the reef to rest in small holes. It is absent from Florida but seen elsewhere throughout the region on reefs from depths of 13 to 105m (43 to 345ft).

8 REDLIP BLENNY
Ophioblennius atlanticus

The redlip blenny gets its name from its large lips that are usually reddish in colour. The front end of the body is darker than the rear end, and the head has a steep profile. This species reaches a length of about 12cm (4¾in). *Ecology*: occurs on rocky and coral reefs throughout the region, usually in shallow water, but may be found to depths of 40m (130ft). It is territorial and not afraid of divers. It often rests on the bottom on its pelvic fins.

GOBIES
FAMILY GOBIIDAE

Gobies are small fish with elongate bodies. They are sometimes confused with blennies, but can be recognised by the two dorsal fins and also by the rather stiff way that they hold their bodies. Blennies have a single dorsal fin and the body tends to be flexed when the fish is resting. Most gobies are bottom dwellers, and they often balance on their pelvic and pectoral fins. The pelvic fins are generally modified into a small sucking disk, which keeps the fish securely in place in areas of strong water movement. As many as 40 species may occur on and around reefs in the area – a few of the commonest and most easily identified are illustrated here. Most gobies can be approached quite closely, and the cleaner species may even investigate divers' fingers if they are kept very still.

7 BARSNOUT GOBY
Gobiosoma illecebrosum

The barsnout goby has a white bar that runs from between the eye down to the upper lip. Both the head and body are darkish brown and there is a long pale blue or yellowish line running along each side of the body. It reaches a maximum length of about 4.5cm (1¾in). *Ecology*: restricted to the western and southern Caribbean, occurring on reefs at depths of 10 to 30m (33 to 98ft). This species is a cleaner and often gathers in small groups at cleaning stations, waiting for clients.

6 Secretary Blenny

7 Arrow Blenny

8 Redlip Blenny

1 Barsnout Goby

2 CLEANING GOBY
Gobiosoma genie

This species has a bright yellow V-shape on the head that continues into a paler yellow stripe running down the length of the body. It reaches a maximum length of about 4.5cm (1¾in). *Ecology*: restricted to the Bahamas and Caribbean where it is common on reefs from shallow water to depths of about 15m (49ft). This species is a cleaner and often gathers in small groups at cleaning stations, waiting for clients. All the cleaners have a bright line running along the body which advertises their presence and makes them recognisable to the clients. They move rapidly about on the surface of the fish they are cleaning, keeping a grip by using the suction disk on the pelvic fin. Their small size enables them to get right inside the client's mouth and gill cavities.

3 SHARKNOSE GOBY
Gobiosoma evelynae

Gobiosoma evelynae also has a V-shape on the snout. Its body colour is very variable, from pale to bright yellow, and the stripe ranges from yellow to light blue. The pale yellow form is very similar to *G. genie*. It reaches a maximum length of about 3.8cm (1½in). *Ecology*: occurs on reefs throughout the region, from shallow water to depths of about 50m (165ft). This species is a cleaner and often gathers in small groups at cleaning stations, waiting for clients.

4 NEON GOBY
Gobiosoma oceanops

The neon goby has a bright blue stripe running along each side of the body from just in front of the eye to the base of the tail. Unlike the sharknose and cleaner goby, the mouth of the neon goby is terminal rather than 'underslung'. It reaches a maximum length of about 5cm (2in). *Ecology*: absent from the Bahamas and Caribbean islands, but common in Florida and along the western islands and mainland. This species is a cleaner and often gathers in small groups at cleaning stations, waiting for clients.

5 ORANGESIDED GOBY
Gobiosoma dilepsis

This species has distinctive orange-red dashes running along each side of the body, and several squarish, orange marks at the front end of the body. The fins and rear end of the body are nearly transparent. It is one of the smallest gobies, seldom exceeding 2.5cm (1in) in length. *Ecology*: absent from Florida and rare elsewhere, occurring on reefs from shallow water to depths of about 30m (98ft) where it may be spotted perching on the surface of corals and sponges.

6 COLON GOBY
Coryphopterus dicrus

This species has a very pale body speckled with tiny reddish-brown spots. It has two darker, larger spots in front of the pectoral fin base, and another two at the base of the tail, which may be joined together. It reaches a maximum length of about 5cm (2in). *Ecology*: occurs throughout the region, especially on shallow sandy and rubble patches adjacent to reefs. It blends in with the background and is easily overlooked.

7 BRIDLED GOBY
Coryphopterus glaucofraenum

The bridled goby has a whitish to transparent body with occasional yellowish dots and markings. There is a dark spot above the gill cover and a streak running from this spot to the eye. It reaches a maximum length of about 5cm (2in). *Ecology*: occurs in sandy habitats in the vicinity of reefs. It is abundant throughout the region from shallow water to depths of about 40m (130ft). This species is unafraid although will dart away if divers make a sudden, close approach.

2 Cleaning Goby

3 Sharknose Goby

4 Neon Goby

5 Orangesided Goby

6 Colon Goby

7 Bridled Goby

8 PEPPERMINT GOBY
Coryphopterus lipernes

This species has a pale or translucent body with gold markings and bright blue tinges on the head. It grows to a length of about 3cm (1¼in). *Ecology*: absent from the Bahamas, but seen occasionally on reefs in other areas, from shallow water to depths of about 40m (130ft). Like a number of other gobies, it spends much of its time perched on coral heads, on the look out for small planktonic prey. It usually remains still in the presence of divers, but will skip rapidly to a new vantage point if too close an approach is made.

9 MASKED GOBY
Coryphopterus personatus

The masked goby is translucent with a darkish mark on the front of the head, brightish-orange anterior body and a row of small white dashes along each side of the body. It grows to a length of about 3.8cm (1½in). *Ecology*: common throughout the region, from shallow water to depths of about 30m (98ft). This species is found in coral reefs, sandy and seagrass habitats. Individuals aggregate in small or large groups, and hover just above the seabed.

SURGEONFISH
FAMILY ACANTHURIDAE

Surgeonfish have an oval-shaped, compressed body, a small mouth and a long, continuous dorsal fin. They get their name from the scalpel-like spine on each side of the tail stem. These are used both for offence and defence, including territorial defence against others of their own species. Surgeonfish are important herbivores and often feed in the shallowest regions of the reef front.

Other surgeonfish occur in aggregations and sometimes in huge shoals. Often the shoals are mixed species, and it is thought that species massing together in this way may do so in order to be able to compete better with dominant, territorial competitors for algae.

1 OCEAN SURGEONFISH
Acanthurus bahianus

The colour of the ocean surgeonfish can change in an instant from pale grey to dark brown. There may be a white bar across the tail stem and bluish markings on the face. It reaches a maximum length of about 38cm (1ft 3in). *Ecology*: common on rocky and coral reefs throughout the region, from shallow water to depths of about 20m (66ft). It is sometimes solitary, but more often occurs in aggregations that may also include blue tangs and the similar looking doctorfish (*A. chirurgus*). The latter is distinguished by the presence of a series of dark bars on the body.

2 BLUE TANG
Acanthurus coeruleus

Adults of this species are overall blue in colour, but can change rapidly from pale to dark according to their mood and habitat. They are deep bodied with small, pointed mouths, and reach a maximum length of about 38cm (1ft 3in). Juveniles may be bright blue with a yellow tail, or completely yellow except for the fins' margins and eyes, which are blue. *Ecology*: common on rocky and coral reefs throughout the region, from shallow water to depths of about 20m (66ft). It is sometimes solitary, but more often occurs in large aggregations.

8 Peppermint Goby

9 Masked Goby

1 Ocean Surgeonfish

2 Blue Tang (juvenile)

2 Blue Tang (adult)

FLOUNDERS
FAMILY BOTHIDAE

1 PEACOCK FLOUNDER
Bothus lunatus

A number of species out of this large family are seen in the vicinity of reefs. The peacock flounder has a number of scattered dark blotches on the body, but is positively identified by the numerous blue rings and the blue spots on the head. This species can change colour rapidly so that it always blends in with its background. Even though the blue marks fade, they can still just be made out. Like other flounders, *Bothus lunatus* has both eyes on the left side of the head. The eye from the right side migrates round as the fish develops from the free swimming juvenile to take up a bottom-dwelling existence. *Ecology*: occurs throughout the region, mainly in shallow sandy, rubble and seagrass habitats. It is often partially buried in sand and may occasionally be seen on rocks. If care is taken, it can be approached quite closely.

TRIGGERFISH
FAMILY BALISTIDAE

Triggerfish have fairly deep, compressed bodies with eyes set high on the head. The skin is tough and covered with non-overlapping scales which act a bit like armour plating. They get their name from the large, first dorsal spine, which can be erected and then locked into place by the second smaller spine which fits neatly into a groove in the first spine. When not in use, these spines are folded away so may not be visible. The locking strategy enables the fish to wedge themselves into crevices if threatened by predators. Triggerfish have a small mouth. Most feed on shelled animals such as crustaceans, molluscs and sea urchins, which they can easily crush with their powerful jaws and teeth. A few feed on plankton. Most triggerfish occur singly, but have conspicuous colour patterns and so are easily picked out. They also have a curious way of swimming: by undulating the anal and second dorsal fin, bringing in the tail for an extra turn of speed.

1 QUEEN TRIGGERFISH
Balistes vetula

The colour of the queen triggerfish is variable, but cannot be confused with any other species. It is a flamboyant mixture of yellow, green and blue, which may be light or dark according to the fish's mood. It reaches a maximum length of about 60cm (2ft). *Ecology*: occurs throughout the region on reefs and adjacent sandy and rubble areas from shallow water to depths of 50m (165ft). It has a particular liking for the long-spined sea urchin *Diadema antillarum*, which it attacks by blowing water under it to overturn it so that it can launch an attack where the spines are shortest.

2 BLACK DURGON
Melichthys niger

The body of this species is usually overall dark, but it can become paler. There are prominent thin white lines running along the base of the anal and dorsal fins. It reaches a maximum length of about 50cm (1ft 8in). *Ecology*: the black durgon is one of the few reef species to occur throughout both the tropical Indo-Pacific and the western Atlantic. It occurs in small aggregations from shallow water to depths of 60m (195ft), feeding mainly on large zooplankton and floating algal debris. At night it retires to shelter holes, often using the same one for months at a time.

1 Peacock Flounder

1 Queen Triggerfish

2 Black Durgon

1 OCEAN TRIGGERFISH

Canthidermis sufflamen

This species is uniform grey in colour with a dark spot at the base of the pectoral fin. It reaches a maximum length of about 60cm (2ft). *Ecology*: occurs around reefs throughout the region, from depths of 12 to 40m (39 to 130ft). It is usually alone or in small groups in open water and is more likely to be encountered when it is nesting. All triggerfish make a nest and lay eggs on the seabed. They do this by excavating a depression in the sand and rubble, depositing eggs and sperm and then vigorously defending the developing eggs. At this time they will chase away divers if they approach too closely.

FILEFISH
FAMILY MONACANTHIDAE

Filefish (also known as leatherjackets) are closely related to triggerfish but have a longer, thinner first dorsal spine, which cannot be locked up. The scales are also much smaller, and these are covered with small hairs (setae) which give the surface a rough texture like a file. There is also usually a patch of longer setae on each side of the body, just in front of the tail stem. These hairs are better developed in males, and may bear small hooks. Another feature of filefish is that they are able to change colour to match their surroundings, which triggerfish cannot do.

1 SCRAWLED FILEFISH

Aluterus scriptus

This species has a characteristic shape, with an elongate tail. The body colour varies but there are always blue lines and spots, with a scattering of black spots. It reaches a maximum length of about 110cm (3ft 7in). *Ecology*: the scrawled filefish is found in tropical waters throughout the world, and is usually seen drifting over reefs a few feet above the bottom. It occurs from shallow water to depths of about 80m (260ft) and feeds on a range of reef organisms including algae, seagrass and gorgonians.

2 WHITESPOTTED FILEFISH

Cantherhines macrocerus

This species gets its name from the numerous large white spots that cover the body. But confusingly, there is also an orange-brown phase in which the spots do not show. Positive identification is usually possible by looking at the base of the tail, where there are two small orange spines. This species reaches a maximum length of 42cm (1ft 5in). *Ecology*: occurs around reefs throughout the region, from depths of 5 to 25m (16 to 82ft). It quite often moves around in pairs, searching for food such as sponges, algae and gorgonians.

3 SLENDER FILEFISH

Monocanthus tuckeri

The slender filefish is a small species, maximum length about 10cm (4in), with a relatively long snout. It has a brown and white reticulated pattern, which may become rather indistinct as the fish changes colour to blend in with the background. *Ecology*: occurs throughout the region on reefs, seagrass beds and rubble areas to a depth of about 20m (66ft). It often associates with gorgonians, and may be difficult to spot because of its effective camouflage. It feeds on algae and small invertebrates.

3 Ocean Triggerfish

1 Scrawled Filefish

2 Whitespotted Filefish

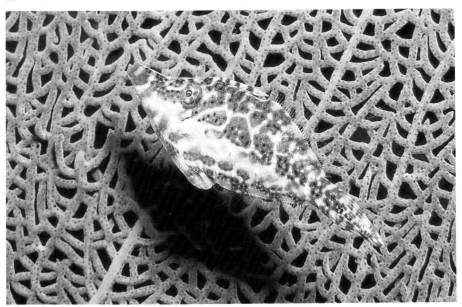

3 Slender Filefish

TRUNKFISH
FAMILY OSTRACIIDAE

These fish get their name from the bony plates that encase the head and body. The shell is inflexible and often adorned with ridges and spines. There are small gaps for the mouth, eyes, gill openings, anus and fins. Trunkfish are predators on a range of small invertebrates. Most live in territories consisting of a dominant male with several females and sub-adults. Apart from their protective armoury, many trunkfish also secrete toxic substances when alarmed or threatened. This can be lethal to other fish, especially in the confines of an aquarium.

1 HONEYCOMB COWFISH
Lactophrys polygonia

As its name implies, this species can be recognized by its very distinct honeycomb pattern. Another identification feature is the presence of a small, sharp spine projecting forwards from just above the eye. It reaches a maximum length of 46cm (1ft 6in). *Ecology*: a shy and uncommon species that occurs on reefs throughout the region, from shallow water to depths of about 80m (260ft). It feeds on a variety of invertebrates, including sponges, sea squirts and shrimps.

2 SMOOTH TRUNKFISH
Lactophrys triqueter

This species is greyish with numerous small white spots and a yellowish wash in the middle of the body where there is also a faint honeycomb pattern. It reaches a maximum length of 30cm (12in). The juvenile has a darker background colour and lacks the yellowish honeycomb markings. *Ecology*: occurs throughout the region, on reefs and adjacent sandy areas from shallow water to depths of about 25m (82ft). It feeds on small invertebrates, which it disturbs from the sand by shooting out a jet of water from its mouth.

3 SPOTTED TRUNKFISH
Lactophrys bicaudalis

This distinctive species is white with evenly spaced black spots. It reaches a length of about 40cm (1ft 4in). *Ecology*: occurs on rocky and coral reefs throughout the area, from shallow water to depths of about 20m (66ft). It is quite a shy species and often retreats to small holes and hiding places when approached. It has a mixed diet of sea cucumbers, sea urchins, sea squirts and seagrasses.

4 SCRAWLED COWFISH
Acanthostracion quadricornis

The scrawled cowfish has similar colour patterns to the scrawled filefish, and the two species can sometimes be mistaken at first glance. However, there are a number of distinctive differences. The cowfish has a more rounded body, without the pointed snout, and has a distinctive, small spine above the eye. Finally, the blue lines on the body of the scrawled cowfish are more closely set in a swirling pattern than they are in the filefish. The markings may be more or less obvious depending on the fish's surroundings, because it takes on different hues to blend in with the background. It reaches a maximum length of about 46cm (18"). Ecology: this species is found throughout the region generally on seagrass beds. It may also be seen around reefs, down to depths of about 25m (82ft). It is sometimes overlooked because it is well camouflaged and tends to remain until divers get close. The scrawled cowfish feeds on a range of attached animals such as sponges, seasquirts and anemones.

1 Honeycomb Cowfish

2 Smooth Trunkfish

3 Spotted Trunkfish

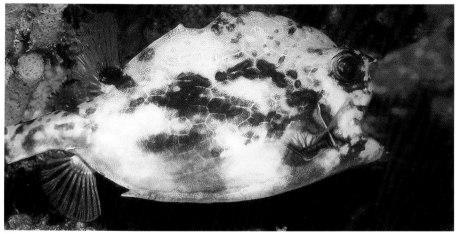

4 Scrawled Cowfish

PUFFERFISH
FAMILY TETTRAODONTIDAE

Pufferfish get their name from the ability to puff up their bodies in self defence by drawing water through the mouth into a special chamber near the stomach. They have tough, prickly skin that is greatly stretched during this process until the fish resembles a small football. If this is not enough to deter predators, pufferfish also contain a powerful toxin in the viscera, gonads and skin. Pufferfish have a mixed diet, including algae, and both hard and soft bodied invertebrates. They hide at night and are active during the day. Divers should never chase or annoy them in order to try and make them inflate.

1 SHARPNOSE PUFFER
Canthigaster rostrata

This species has a more pointed nose than other puffer species. The back is brownish with blue markings, and there are many fine blue lines on the face. It reaches a maximum length of 11cm (4¼in). *Ecology*: occurs on reefs and seagrass beds throughout the region, from shallow water to depths of about 30m (98ft). It feeds on the growing tips of seagrasses, together with a range of invertebrates including sponges, crustaceans and worms.

2 BANDTAIL PUFFER
Sphoeroides spengleri

There is a distinctive broad, white bar on the tail of this species, and a row of brown spots along the length of the body. It reaches a maximum length of 30cm (12in). *Ecology*: commons on reefs and seagrass beds throughout the region, from shallow water to depths of about 30m (98ft). The bandtail puffer is relatively unafraid of divers if approached with care. It feeds on a range of benthic invertebrates.

PORCUPINEFISH
FAMILY DIODONTIDAE

Porcupinefish are very similar to pufferfish. The main difference is that the body is covered in sharp spines (modified scales), which become erect when the body is inflated. They have hard, beak-like jaws well adapted for crushing shelled animals such as molluscs, crustaceans and sea urchins.

1 PORCUPINE FISH
Diodon histrix

Both the body and fins are covered with small black spots. This is a large species, reaching a maximum length of 90cm (3ft). *Ecology*: occurs in tropical waters throughout the world, mainly on coral and rocky reefs from shallow water to depths of about 20m (66ft). It tends to rest under ledges during the day and emerge at night to forage for hard-shelled invertebrates such as crabs and gastropods.

2 BALLOONFISH
Diodon holocanthus

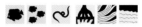

The balloonfish has black blotches and spots on the body, but none on the fins. It reaches a maximum length of about 50cm (1ft 8in). *Ecology*: this species is found in most tropical waters around the world, occurring in a range of habitats including mangrove, seagrass beds and reefs. It is a poor swimmer and moves around slowly in search of hard-shelled invertebrates.

1 Sharpnose Puffer

2 Bandtail Puffer

1 Porcupine Fish

2 Balloonfish

TURTLES

Of the seven species of marine turtle found throughout the world, six can be found in the tropical Atlantic region. Although these reptiles spend long periods submerged, they have to come to the surface to breathe, and females also make their way on to land to lay eggs. When struggling up the beach to nest they look ungainly, yet underwater they are magnificent and powerful swimmers. The shell is good protection, but sometimes bears scars – perhaps from encounters with boat propellers, or with their only natural predator, the shark. Given the chance, turtles are long-lived. They may not reach sexual maturity until they are well over 20 years old, and may live to be over 100 years old. Due to the many pressures on turtles, all species are listed in Appendix I of the *Convention on Trade in Endangered Species*, which prohibits all international trade in them.

1 GREEN TURTLE
Chelonia mydas

The green turtle has a wide, rounded head, non-overlapping bony plates (scutes) on the back and a white underside. Young are carnivorous, but adults feed on seagrasses and seaweeds. Like other turtles, they have a parrot-like beak and strong jaws. This turtle has a world-wide distribution and huge populations used to occur in the western Atlantic, but numbers have been greatly reduced as a result of being hunted for food.

2 HAWKSBILL TURTLE
Eretmochelys imbriocota

This species is distinguished by its pointed head, hawk-like beak, and overlapping bony plates on the back. The richly coloured and patterned shell has been the hawksbill's downfall because of its value for jewellery and objects such as spectacle frames. The hawksbill occurs on coral reefs world-wide, and feeds on attached reef organisms – particularly sponges, which it rips apart with gusto.

DOLPHINS

These warm-blooded, intelligent mammals are a welcome sight as they play alongside boats, or visit the reef, but their real domain is out in the ocean, catching fish. Dolphins do not have a well-developed sense of smell and taste, and their eyesight is relatively poor. They make up for this by having a highly sensitive 'echo-location' system, which enables them to pick up sounds, locate prey and understand precisely what is going on around them. All dolphins have powerful, sleek bodies and strong limbs adapted to form fins.

1 BOTTLENOSE DOLPHIN
Tursiops truncatus

The bottlenose dolphin occurs in all oceans and is one of the species most likely to be encountered. It is quite bulky in comparison with other dolphins and has a short beak which is clearly marked off from the forehead. Bottlenose dolphins are unafraid of humans and some strike up a special relationship, apparently enjoying the company of people rather than their own kind. It is possible that these individuals are outcasts from the dolphin world. Yet under normal circumstances, the bottlenose dolphin is a highly social animal, living in groups of around 15 (sometimes many more), in which individuals assist each other in activities such as feeding and child care. They live for 25–30 years, and begin breeding at the age of about six. Food consists mainly of bottom-dwelling animals such as eels, rays, mullet, shrimps and hermit crabs, but they also catch pelagic fish.

1 Green Turtle

2 Hawksbill Turtle

1 Bottlenose Dolphin

GLOSSARY

Basal plate:
a hard plate at the base of some corals from which individual stalks or branches grow.

Benthic:
bottom dwelling.

Corallite:
the calcium carbonate wall that coral polyps build around themselves for protection.

Drop-off:
the point at which a submarine plateau gives way to a deeper wall.

Phytoplankton:
plankton that live by photosynthesis.

Polyp:
the individual animals that form a coral colony.

Reef flat:
the horizontal part of the reef that usually lies only a few metres from the surface.

Setae:
bristles.

Zooplankton:
larger carnivorous plankton.

INDEX